PERFECT TIME MANAGEMENT

Ted Johns, PhD, MA(Soc), BSc(Econ),
FIPM, ACIS, MIMC, MIM

For the past 25 years Ted Johns has directed The
PROSPER Consortium, a group of consultants
specializing in the improvement of management
performance. During part of that time he was Head
of the Personnel Management Division in the
Business School at Thames Valley University, where
he was responsible for various post-graduate and
post-experience programmes in human resource development, but from 1983 onwards he has concentrated exclusively on his consultancy career.

Ted Johns has written four books, several articles
(for *Management Today* and *Personnel Management*), and for eleven years acted as Managing
Editor for the *Sunridge Park Management Review*.
He devised the *Professional Timekeeper* management diary system, widely used in organizations to
help managers to plan their time more effectively.

Consultancy clients include SmithKline Beecham
Consumer Brands, Philips Electronics, Pearl
Assurance, Unilever and British Aerospace. Apart
from assignments in the UK, Ted Johns has also led
training programmes on mainland Europe and in
the Far East. He is an Examiner for three professional bodies; he has lectured at the universities of
Bradford, Kent, Sussex and Reading. His qualifications include full membership of the Institute of
Management Consultants.

Ted Johns is much in demand as a keynote
speaker at in-company conferences, meetings and
seminars, on topics associated with time management, quality and customer care, transformational
leadership and creative innovation.

OTHER TITLES IN THE SERIES

PERFECT TIME MANAGEMENT

All you need to get it right first time

Ted Johns

RANDOM HOUSE

BUSINESS BOOKS

This edition published in the United Kingdom in 2003
by Random House Business Books

First published in 1994 by Arrow Books
Random House, 20 Vauxhall Bridge Road, London SW1V 2SA

Random House Australia (Pty) Limited
20 Alfred Street, Milsons Point
Sydney, New South Wales 2061, Australia

Random House New Zealand Limited
18 Poland Road, Glenfield
Auckland 10, New Zealand

Random House South Africa (Pty) Limited
Endulini, 5a Jubilee Road, Parktown 2193, South Africa

Random House UK Limited Reg. No. 954009

Papers used by Random House UK Limited are natural, recyclable
products made from wood grown in sustainable forests. The
manufacturing processes conform to the environmental regulations
of the country of origin.

ISBN 1 8441 3157 2

Companies, institutions and other organizations wishing to make
bulk purchases of any business books published by Random House
should contact their local bookstore or Random House direct:
Special Sales Director
Random House, 20 Vauxhall Bridge Road, London SW1V 2SA

Tel: 020 7840 8470 Fax: 020 7828 6681

www.randomhouse.co.uk
businessbooks@randomhouse.co.uk

Typeset in Sabon by SX Composing DTP, Rayleigh, Essex
Printed and bound in Great Britain by
Bookmarque, Croydon, Surrey

Acknowledgements

Authors generally say that they owe an enormous debt to a vast army of people who (whether they knew it or not) have helped firm up, consolidate, reinforce, adapt and improve the writer's original thoughts. In my case some of these people have even caused me to accept that my first ideas were wrong and/or foolish, and so they've prevented me from making an even bigger fool of myself.

If I am forced to name names, then I shall single out some of my former Thames Valley University colleagues like Don Halstead and Arthur Adamson, who taught me a lot about managing the boss and the skills of political survival in corporate life. More recently I have received unstinting help from one of my key associates, Geoff Ribbens, whose contribution has been especially valuable so far as this book's Time Management Checklists are concerned.

Contents

TIME MANAGEMENT CHECKLISTS

Preface

In a sense, there is no such thing as *time* management. All management is time management: the process of managing is about deciding what needs to be done, getting it done (through others), and then reflecting on experience so that an improved planning-doing cycle can begin again. Time management is scarcely any different. If you manage your time effectively, you will be selecting defensible (value-added) objectives and priorities, applying appropriate disciplines in order to make things happen, and then implementing performance improvements.

Furthermore, the skills of time management don't just apply to managers. They are needed by everyone in an organization (and actually by everyone in their ordinary lives as well, when you come to think of it). Even the lowest-level employee can make time-management choices (about trips to the vending machine) which in their own way can be just as disruptive to the organization as inept personal organization on the part of more senior staff. Increasingly, in fact, employees can (and do) work from home, as sales representatives have always done. For such people, the skills of managing time make even more sense, given that they don't have the externally-imposed controls of 'normal' working hours and visible arrival/departure times to push them into channelled behaviour patterns.

What follows in this book reflects the distillation of over twenty years' experience in designing and leading time-management programmes built around the beliefs briefly stated in the above paragraphs.

A further point has to be made. It is one thing to *read* about time-management; it is quite another to *do* it properly. The difference between *knowing* how to do something and being *able* to do it can be quite astounding. If this were not the case, then those who read books about golf would all be world champions. Having read *Perfect Time Management*, you may well decide that you need first-class organization-specific training so that you can apply the ideas, skills and techniques from these pages to the real world of your life and your work. You can contact the author, Ted Johns, at the offices of The PROSPER Consortium, PROSPER House, 30 Waterhouse Mead, Camberley, Surrey GU15 4ZD (telephone 0276-31085) in order to discuss the design and operation of such training. You will be joining companies like SmithKline Beecham Consumer Brands, Pearl Assurance PLC, Unilever, Philips Electronics, British Aerospace and Eastern Electricity.

Dr Ted Johns

Introduction

The issue of good time management, to get the most out of one's career and life, is important not only to managers and executives but to all of us. The real reason for managing time effectively is to allow us to lead as fulfilling a life as possible, to enjoy recreation and allow time to be spent with our families. For example: *we only have one chance to spend time with our children when they are young. If that opportunity isn't taken, tomorrow will be too late.*

When we are young and at the beginning of the work/job/career cycle, we are conditioned to trade our time for money as we build our careers and security for our families. The trap that many of us fall into is that, as we become older and achieve success, we do not reverse the trend. Many of us work harder and longer, giving up even more time for money – or for what?

This book will help you make sense of your situation, of the options available to you, and of the techniques and skills essential to grabbing control of your time and your life.

Philosophically, the book relies strongly on the four essential realities affecting the time constraints for the manager (as outlined in Peter Drucker's *The Effective Executive*):

1. The manager's time belongs to everyone else and tends to be taken away from him in order to give the company direction.
2. The manager is often forced to keep on 'operating' unless he takes positive action to avoid this problem. The effective manager will not allow operational events to control his time as this will divert him from dealing with more important – strategic and value-added – matters.
3. The manager can be distracted because, being part of an organization, he needs to make and maintain relationships with other people in the organization. Without these links, a manager's ability to get things done can be reduced.
4. The manager needs to be aware of what is happening outside the organization if changes need to be made.

The manager's time is continually invaded by seniors, subordinates, internal and external peers, 'customers' from everywhere. They make up what Margol and Kleiner have termed the 'management molecule'. Understanding each part of the molecule is instrumental to becoming a successful manager (defined as one with a good proportion of discretionary time). We believe that relationships with the boss are probably critical determinants for anybody's time management, and therefore subordinates should take the initiative to be a good 'managee'. That is why this book contains a whole chapter about managing the boss.

Also, although we talk a good deal about becoming 'ruthless' and 'disciplined' in dealing with others, none of the material in the following pages should be interpreted as suggesting that positive relationships with others are of little account. On the contrary, the co-operation and goodwill of others is *vital* to our effective time management. Take this example (cited by Margol and Kleiner):

Manager A and Manager B are both sales managers in their companies. It is 15 minutes before closing and Manager A needs 200 copies of a new order form for his sales meeting tomorrow morning. He calls the copy room but the copy person [the internal peer] refuses to make the copies as company policy requires a lead time of 24 hours for quantities over 50 copies. Manager A is out of luck and will be that much less effective at his meeting tomorrow.

Manager B needs the same 200 copies for her meeting tomorrow. She calls the copy room 5 minutes later with the same request but this time the copy person says the 200 copies *will* be ready in 10 minutes.

The moral is that internal peers, if not managed properly, can extend the time it takes to do a job. Manager A has a low credit rating with the copy person but Manager B has a high credit rating and is able to get round company policy to obtain her copies in 10 minutes. Managers need to develop high credit ratings with internal peers. Neglect this advice at your peril.

Now read on.

CHAPTER 1

Why Bother About Managing Time?

The simple answer to this essential question is that if you don't manage your time (i.e., you don't *take control of what you do with your time*), then:

- **You'll be inefficient:** the things you do will take longer than is necessary; you'll make more mistakes; you will lose things, miss deadlines; your workstation area will be a mess.
- **You'll be ineffective:** the difference between efficiency and effectiveness is that the first is concerned with *inputs* and the second is to do with *outputs*. Managers, like everybody else, are paid for their *outputs*, i.e., what they achieve and (increasingly) the degree to which they can add value for their employer. If you're inefficient it's very unlikely that you will be effective – as we shall see later, effectiveness is all about Performance Improvement and Managing Change.
- **You won't get promotion** – because you'll be wasting time on activities which don't get you noticed, or which get you noticed in the worst possible way (e.g., by missing deadlines).
- **You've a good chance of being made redundant,** especially in those large-scale shake-outs when

'redundancy' is a euphemism for 'getting rid of people who aren't any good'.

- **Your subordinates (if you have any) won't be able to do their jobs properly** because you won't be supplying them with leadership or guidance when it's needed, and your priorities will be unpredictable.
- **Your boss will come to regard you as a waste of space:** you are disorganized, you make mistakes, you lose things, you can't answer questions, your work is poorly presented.

And so it goes on: a vicious circle of incompetence, inadequacy, inefficiency and ineffectiveness. Is this an exaggeration? No, it is not. Is it fair to place so much of a central focus on the issue of managing time? Yes, it is, a thousand times.

Time Isn't Like the Brazilian Rain Forest

The Brazilian rain forest can be replaced: time is irreplaceable. Once today is finished, it cannot be reused, we can't have a second go at it. We can only hope that tomorrow will enable us to learn and apply the lessons of today.

The situation is made worse by the fact that you only have a limited amount of time left. Nobody knows in advance, of course, precisely how much time they have (this is probably a good thing), but for each one of us the supply is undoubtedly limited. Shouldn't we be making the best of this time, then?

Time Isn't Like a Table-Tennis Ball

The typical manager has one hour alone each day, if he's lucky. Even that hour isn't a continuous 60 minutes, but comprises fragmentary periods of solitude. The frequency of interruptions, and their nature, depends on the managerial role (and how he chooses to perform it), but in general the interruptions occur every eight minutes or so, and typically take the form of subordinates seeking advice, instructions or decisions (we call this the 'AID' syndrome).

According to Eric Webster (*How to Win the Business Battle*), the manager 'devotes 80 per cent of time to "communicating" and only 18½ per cent to "creative work". In other words he spends more time talking than thinking, tends to be run by his business instead of running it, and has about as much mastery over his environment as a table-tennis ball.'

Elsewhere, George Copeman has argued that 'By and large, a cut of between one quarter and one fifth in the time an executive spends per week seeing people, writing to them, phoning, reading reports and so forth, can mean doubling the time available for creative work and possibly doubling his effectiveness as an executive.'

So time management is important: it creates opportunities for you to do the things you should really be doing, instead of constantly fire-fighting and running round like a headless chicken.

MANAGING TIME MEANS ADDING VALUE

Everybody's job in any organization is a combination of four roles:

1. **Maintenance**: fire-fighting and trouble-shooting – making sure that at the end of each day the situation is no worse than it was at the beginning.
2. **Crisis Prevention**: creating an environment with the minimum of surprise, by (a) preventing the recurrence of previously-encountered 'crises', and (b)

anticipating future 'crises' in order to prevent them from happening or minimise their impact when or if they do strike.

3. **Performance Improvement:** doing current things better (to a higher standard of quality), faster (to tighter deadlines, with shorter delivery dates) or cheaper (using fewer resources of all kinds: people, money, space, hardware and software).

4. **Managing Change:** introducing new ideas and translating them into tangible results for the benefit of the business and the organization.

If you are serious about adding value to your organization, this means spending less time on Maintenance and Crisis Prevention, because these activities (though essential) do not add value: they simply ensure that value remains the same, i.e., that things continue at their present level of quality, speed and cost. In other words, Maintenance and Crisis Prevention are exclusively about *efficiency*, not effectiveness: you can be quite good at Maintenance and Crisis Prevention, but no matter how good you are at doing the things associated with Maintenance and Crisis Prevention, *you will never add value to your organization.*

Now, this revelation may not bother you that much, but it should, because increasingly *all* organizations nowadays are looking for added-value out of *all* their employees. It's worth restating this proposition: *the concept of adding value applies to everyone working in an organization, not just managers.* At one time, concentrating exclusively on Maintenance, without even any Crisis Prevention thrown in, was regarded as acceptable, especially for lower-level workers: they could spend all their time fire-fighting and trouble-shooting, and everyone (including themselves) would think this was what their jobs were about. **This is no longer the case.** Techniques like TQM embody the principle that everybody must devote some time to thinking about how they could do their jobs better – in other words, how they could **add value.**

If you, working with your organization, can find ways of spending less time on Maintenance – much of the time devoted to Maintenance arises because previous mistakes have to be corrected: so getting it 'right first time' (an essential principle for TQM) would by itself release enormous quantities of time for more productive purposes – then you have much greater opportunities for adding value by looking at your job creatively, purposefully, proactively.

The first thing to do, before we get down to some of the everyday issues about time management, is to generate a **mission statement** for your role which emphasizes your **value-added contribution.** This mission statement should:

- Have no more than about six words – ten at the most – so that it is easily memorable.
- Begin with an upward-sounding verb which implies the notion of added value: 'to improve', 'to develop', 'to maximize', 'to optimize' rather than 'to maintain', 'to ensure', 'to prevent'.
- Be free of 'job-description-speak': that pseudo-impressive language which often appears in bureaucratic documents about job descriptions, where everything is hedged about with qualifications, caveats, conditional clauses and adverbial phrases like 'other things being equal'.

You need a mission statement of this kind because it will then help you make defensible judgements about

8

priorities when managing your time. In an ideal world, you'd keep your mission statement permanently in front of you, in a picture frame on the wall, or carved into your desk, so that you're always reminding yourself about why you exist as an employee of your organization. We shall refer to the mission statement several times, later in this book: it helps to select sensible Key Tasks, it helps when deciding what to do and what not to do, and it helps in communicating a sense of purpose to any others who work for you.

Here are some examples of mission statements for various organizational roles:

For a sales manager: 'To maximize profitable sales for my product or area.'

For a maintenance manager: 'To improve machine utilization uptime.'

For a personnel manager: 'To develop the productivity of the organization's employees.'

Everyone can produce a value-added mission statement for their role. If you can't, it's probably because you aren't thinking of your role in sufficiently value-added terms. Even if your role seems to be a purely policing, preventative function in the organization (e.g., you're in charge of a Compliance Unit in a financial services company), you can still express your purpose in value-added terms, because you can find ways of achieving your objectives more proactively – by 'crime prevention', as it were – or by achieving the same standards with fewer resources (this could be the measure of Performance Improvement for you).

If, after all your efforts, you can't think of any way in which you could add value in your role, then get ready for redundancy. Sooner or later somebody will find out that you don't add value, and your days will be numbered.

All of this talk about adding value is designed to drag managers – and all other employees, for that matter – away from the comfortable belief that efficient trouble-shooting and fire-fighting are what time management is actually about. So let's just spend a moment examining precisely why such a belief could be mistaken.

The trouble-shooter is a person who spends most of the day dealing with crises. His workload is very fragmented, with a great many short-term interruptions. He is reactive rather than proactive. **He considers each day a good one if, at the end of it, the situation is no more than marginally worse than it was at the beginning.**

In our experience, far too many people in organizations (especially managers) perform in trouble-shooter mode. Some do so more or less legitimately, because the job was designed that way. If your role is to sit at a desk dealing with customer complaints, then you can only perform that role when you get complaints (on the other hand, if you're managing a customer complaints facility, you can do a lot to try to eliminate the causes which lead to customer complaints).

Other people operate as trouble-shooters because it has never occurred to them to function in any other way. Some managers see their task simply to survive from one day to the next, dealing with immediate operational problems but devoting scant attention to longer-term issues.

A certain group of managers are trouble-shooters because they are emotionally addicted to a macho image of management in which they are conquering heroes slaying the enemy on a daily basis. It never occurs to them that prolonged excitement may be enjoyable but is ultimately dangerous for survival.

A much larger group of managers are trouble-shooters in spite of themselves. They would like to have more time to think, but don't know how to break out of the vicious circle in which they find themselves: a vicious circle whose highlights include the inability to generate policies/procedures/systems/routines that would save time, because of the time which has to be spent on resolving immediate crises and problems, which are in turn the inevitable consequence of the absence of policies/procedures/systems/routines.

Whether you're a trouble-shooter because you think you have to be, or because you've hitherto thought you want to be, or because it's never occurred to you to be anything else, or because you don't know how to be anything else, then this book is dedicated to you: here are some escape routes (short of suicide, which is one way out).

CHAPTER 2

Four Assumptions About Time Management

Assumption 1: Time can be managed

This assumption may sound daft, but what we're trying to do here is to distinguish between *managing* time and *controlling* time. Very few people can honestly claim that they have total control over their time because, whether you like it or not, some things are going to take you by surprise. The purpose of time management disciplines, then, is to reduce this element of surprise to a minimum, thereby releasing time for more productive (value-added) use.

In practice, the way people operate in organizations can be classified along a continuum between 'Open Door' and 'Closed Door' extremes, with a 'Happy Medium' in the middle:

OPEN DOOR ←———— HAPPY MEDIUM ————→ CLOSED DOOR

Before we go any further, let's make it clear that the phrases 'Open Door' and 'Closed Door' in this continuum are not to be taken literally. It is possible to have a 'Closed Door' management style whether you have a door (and an office of your own) or not: all you have to do is to build up other barriers, like positioning your workstation so that you face the wall and not your visitors, constructing a mountain of files in front of you, or simply by behaving in a curt, dismissive fashion and avoiding eye contact. Equally, you can have an all-comers-are-welcome 'Open Door' mentality even if your office door is physically closed: you simply develop a reputation for inviting interruptions. In fact it's quite rare nowadays for many people to have their own offices, unless they are very senior or perform roles (e.g., personnel officers) where confidential meetings and interviews are regularly required; but this does not invalidate the 'Open Door' and 'Closed Door' continuum. We even know of one company which has physically removed the doors to all its offices, taken them away and burned them, in an effort to create a more 'Open Door' mentality; but of course it has made no difference, because the doors are still there, figuratively speaking.

Our contention is that **unrestricted 'Open Door' and 'Closed Door' policies are disastrous.**

The trouble with an 'Open Door' policy, despite its superficial attractiveness, is that it reduces your ability to control your time to negligible proportions, though it will ensure your continued popularity. Indeed, an 'Open Door' policy carries the seeds of your own destruction because the fact that you willingly accept all interruptions will itself encourage further interruptions, and so on, until your life is an unceasing barrage of gratuitous interruptions – but not much else.

A 'Closed Door' policy, on the other hand, is equally disastrous because, although it gives you almost perfect *control* over your time, it insulates you from what is going on, it isolates you from people who are useful to you, and it prevents you from communicating actively with your own people as much as you should. In some old-fashioned companies, even today, senior managers hide behind solid doors, in privacy and solitude, with the 'traffic-light' signals on their outer wall glowing permanently red. They're getting on with their work, as they see it, but they're certainly not performing adequately as managers of people.

Somewhere in between the twin disasters of 'Open Door' and 'Closed Door' philosophies is the happy medium: you impose your will on events and do not allow yourself to be completely dominated by your work-flow. You allow some people to have access to you, but not everybody; you have times when you arrange to be left alone (barring life-or-death); you have times when you deliberately walk round the place and make yourself visible.

Assumption 2: Work can be made to contract to liberate time not available

This is the corollary of Parkinson's Law, which states that work expands to fill time available. At one time there were managers (and others) for whom Parkinson's Law actually made sense, because their time management problem (if they recognized one at all) was how to drag out what little they had to do so that they could appear to be performing in a worthwhile fashion. Nowadays there is virtually nobody who can make such claims (or would be foolish enough to admit, out loud, that they didn't have enough to do). On the contrary, there are significant pressures which cause managers (and everybody else) to have much more to do. These include:

- 'Empowerment' strategies which give managers a more rounded job with greater accountabilities.
- Flattened hierarchies, with whole strata of middle

management layers being eliminated, therefore creating bigger jobs and a wider span of control for those who remain.

- Much increased competitive pressures, arising from entrepreneurial foreign companies (e.g., in the car and consumer electronics industries) opening up on British soil, the relaxation of inter-country trading controls, the popularity of privatization in what was once the public sector, and so forth.
- Widespread introduction of managerial control and motivational systems designed to concentrate on added value, e.g., performance-related pay, TQM.

There are always two ways in which people can cope with these increasing pressures. One is to manage time much more effectively and productively; the other is simply to elongate the working week, in other words, to remain as efficient (or inefficient) as before, but to tackle increasing accountabilities and demands by coming to work early, staying late, taking work home, working at weekends. Unfortunately this has a number of drawbacks:

- It is a short-term, fire-fighting strategy and in itself it solves nothing.
- It ultimately proves self-defeating as the pressures continue to increase, because there is a finite limit to the number of hours in a week.
- It generates unwanted stress and tensions because of overwork and also countervailing pressures from marriage partners and children, who perceive themselves to be neglected and unwanted, thereby generating a generous dollop of guilt in the luckless manager.

- To cap it all, the positive time manager will say: **It isn't the hours you put in, it's what you put into the hours** which determines whether you're effective or not.

There is ample evidence that despite all these drawbacks, managers in the 1990s are working significantly longer hours. In 1988, for example, British Telecom carried out a small survey involving 140 senior managers. Here are some of the more significant results:

- 54% work more than 10 hours a day
- 71% take work home regularly
- 75% dream about the job
- 75% said that worries about work keep them awake
- 57% had cancelled a holiday or weekend away because of work pressures.

Has it got to be this way? The answer is an emphatic NO. There is no justification for the apparent belief that the longer you work, the more effective you are – indeed, if anything, the reverse if more likely to be true (up to a point: otherwise we might find ourselves arguing that the manager who works one hour a week is super-effective for that reason alone). What counts (or should count) in judging people at work is whether they achieve value-added results – and the number of hours they put in is only one of several factors contributing to this outcome. However, the situation in real life, as opposed to management theory, is complicated by the operation of our third assumption about time management.

Assumption 3: Your effectiveness depends on the extent to which you are seen to be effective, not whether you are actually effective
Let's be quite sure here of what we're saying. Strictly

speaking, a manager's effectiveness is measured by the achievement of value-added results, but there are several reasons why this idealistic prescription is seldom, if ever, accurate.

- Many managers don't have clear-cut objectives which enable their results to be definitively assessed.
- Most managers are themselves managed by bosses whose criteria of effectiveness include not only the achievement of results but also such subjective considerations as whether the subordinate manager operates in the same way as the boss, whether his desk is neat and tidy, and whether he is seen as 'likeable' (i.e., the same sort of person as the boss thinks he is).
- If you work in an organizatioin where it is part of the culture to work late every evening, then you will not be viewed as effective if you leave work 'on time' whatever that might mean). On the contrary, you will be judged to be lazy, lacking in commitment and motivation, when compared with managers who regularly stay late. *This will be true despite the fact that staying late may not be correlated with 'real' effectiveness.*
- Some bosses believe that 'an empty desk indicates a tidy mind', while others argue that 'an empty desk indicates an empty mind'. If you want to be seen to be effective, it may be politically advisable to adapt your work practices to fit in with the known preference of your seniors – even if, in so doing, your behaviour contradicts some of the textbook abstractions about effective time management.

What this boils down to is that there are two meanings for the term 'effectiveness' when applied to a manager (or anyone else):

- You're effective if you do a good job (i.e., you achieve some value-added objectives).
- You're effective if you're seen to be doing a good job (i.e., you achieve some value-added objectives in a manner which fits in with the values, prejudices and idiosyncrasies of your boss and of the organizational culture as a whole).

These two interpretations of 'effectiveness' can be arranged schematically in four different combinations:

	'Real' Effectiveness: doing a good job	Perceived Effectiveness: being seen to be doing a good job
1	√	√
2	√	X
3	X	√
4	X	X

It is our belief that the first of these is preferable to any of the other three. If you can be effective and also be seen to be effective, then:

- You've a better chance of being promoted (because to be promoted you have to be viewed as effective by those who are making the promotion decisions); and
- You've a smaller chance of losing your job in any redundancy shake-outs (for more or less the same reasons).

- You will be able to live with yourself because you'll know that you're doing a good job. By contrast, if you were in category (3), your self-esteem could take a hammering because you would know, in your heart of hearts, that you weren't half as good as other people think you are.

What does all this mean for your time management? Well, it means that you should still manage your time in accordance with the principles, practices and techniques outlined in the book: you should still concentrate on your value-added mission, your key tasks which cluster around the attainment of that mission, and the objectives which enable performance improvement in your key results to be measured. You should still be personally efficient, discriminating about what you do with your time, selective about who has direct access to you, and disciplined in apportioning time to your high-priority and low-priority activities. *But* you have to be aware at all times of the political realities within your organization, sensitive to the corporate culture, attuned to the values of those fallible human beings who make judgements about you (based on their perceptions of your performance, rather than on your performance as such), especially where these judgements can influence your career, your prospects and your job security. To adhere rigorously to the prescriptions in this book could be dangerous if you're working in an organization where the majority of senior people hold different views (however misguided they may be). You can try to change their views, of course, but in the short term you have to live in the real world. Unfortunately the ranks of the redundant are often composed (as some recent research in the UK and the USA tells us) of people who:

- Are uninhibited, unconventional, forthright
- Are not self-critical or self-aware
- Lack political and social skills
- (As a result) made themselves unpopular with senior managers.

It makes some sense, therefore, in a time of turbulence and uncertainty in the labour market, to tailor your time management approaches so that they don't clash with any conflicting ideas held by key players in your organization.

Another critical issue concerns what you have to do if you're ambitious and want career advancement. Clearly this is where the need to be seen to be effective (by those making the promotion decisions) is paramount: so how do you go about this? The first (and most honourable) way is to develop a reputation for adding value: for constantly improving your own performance and that of your group/team/department, for having ideas, for managing change positively and productively. In other words, you manage your time so that you concentrate on these things rather than on any 'comfort zone' of familiar tasks and processes which you can perform without stretching yourself unduly.

The second way of helping in your drive for advancement is to get yourself known by those who are making the promotion decisions: by conspicuous networking, in other words. You can do this by volunteering for project/task groups which give you visibility, by giving presentations to in-company audiences, by constantly putting forward ideas for change and improvement, and by generally walking around the place. Of course, all this takes time, which means you've got to make time for it: but all the research supports the view that those who get on in organizations are the very people who are outward-looking rather than inward-looking.

The Fred Luthans study, *Real Managers* (1988), for example, found a distinction between

- *Effective Managers* – defined by Luthans as managers who got results and whose subordinates liked them; and
- *Successful Managers* – simply those characterized by speed of career advancement within their organizations.

What separated these two groups was the way they allocated their time between the four principal spheres of management, as the following table demonstrates.

	Effective Managers	Successful Managers
Routine Communications Paperwork, administration, Exchanging information	45%	28%
Traditional Management Planning, controlling, decision-making	27%	13%
Networking Interacting with others, socializing and politicking	15%	48%
Human Resource Management Managing conflict, motivating, staffing, disciplining, training and development	12%	11%

So it appears that the ambitious managers devoted *nearly half their time to networking*, whereas the inward-looking effective managers, who got results but not much else, spent *nearly half their time on routine communications and administration*. There is an important lesson here, so don't ignore the implications if you seriously want promotion.

Assumption 4: The secret is to work smarter, not work harder
Nothing in this book is directed at making you work more strenuously to the point where you're more exhausted at the end of the day than you are already. On the contrary, effective time management is about not dissipating your personal resources, it's about concentrating on the essentials and adding value for your organization.

You could do worse than take note of the conscript classification system allegedly used by the Prussian general, Von Moltke (and certainly used by Montgomery during World War II). Based on the assumption that people are a mixture of brains and energy, we can produce the following set of options.

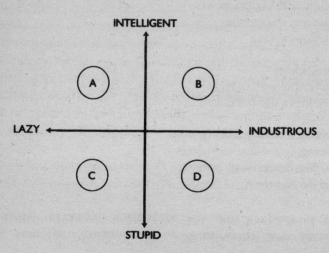

People in quadrant A can be earmarked for top management, not because they use their intelligence in order to do as little as possible, but rather because they are *ingenious* at finding *energy-economical* ways of achieving their objectives: they focus single-mindedly on the genuine priorities. People in quadrant B typically work very hard, but may not achieve so much: they spend much of their time running in order to stand still, allowing themselves to be driven by fire-fighting and crisis management, but not adding value in the process.

Quadrant C is occupied by individuals who have to be confined to simple and menial tasks, preferably where their activities are dictated by, say, the speed of a machine (otherwise their innate laziness will slow them down). Quadrant D inhabitants must be taken out and shot at the earliest opportunity on the grounds that they are highly dangerous: there is no more worrying sight than that of an employee who is stupid but keen.

Quadrant B is the traditional refuge of the workaholic: the individual who has no interests other than his work, who spends many hours actually at work, and who never switches off. Many workaholics become self-employed entrepreneurs, where their unremitting efforts actually become a source of personal gain (though often at the expense of their personal lives). Workaholics do no harm to anyone (except their families) so long as they are only working for themselves, but as soon as they become managers then their addictive intoxication for work becomes a self-evident handicap. Why? Because:

- Workaholics never say 'No' to tasks they are given, no matter how impossible the objectives or the deadline.
- They never say 'Yes' to colleagues or subordinates who offer to help out.

- They are poor delegators: delegation would lessen their workload and they are afraid that the job would be done less well.
- Workaholics develop a reputation for getting things done, so even more tasks are given to them, until eventually they are forced to delegate (however much heartache it causes them) or they crack up under the pressure.
- They devote little attention to training and developing their staff, and then castigate them for being 'incompetent'. In fact, middle managers under a workaholic senior manager are often frustrated, under-employed, rudderless and alienated.

So this fourth assumption is not designed to turn you into a workaholic, but rather to bring you away from the brink of becoming one. If you carry out a personal time analysis [see Chapter 11], you'll know what your specific time management problems are. Then you can set some sensible time-planning objectives. The following are some examples drawn from the author's experience with time management workshops in a variety of companies and organizations – whether they apply to you will depend, of course, on the degree to which the pot and the kettle are both black.

- To reduce my working week by 15 hours (from 70 hours to 55 hours).
- To reduce the number of interruptions by 50 per cent.
- To reduce the time spent on telephone calls by 50 per cent.
- To reduce the time spent on correspondence and administration by 30 per cent.

- To double the time allotted for planning and thinking (so that I set aside not less than one half-day each week – 10 per cent of my available time – for this purpose).
- To spend not less than 10 per cent of my time in Management By Walking Around (MBWA) so that I increase my networking skills and my leadership behaviour.
- To reduce the length of my meetings from an average of three hours to an average of two hours.
- To reduce the number of meetings I attend by 50 per cent (principally by delegating attendance to others).
- To delegate responsibilities and authority more systematically to people in my team.
- To be more rigorous in restricting access to myself, through the use of 'surgery hours' and other devices.

CHAPTER 3

Typical Time Management Issues

Everybody has his own particular time management difficulties. Here are 13 of the most common causes. If you've carried out a personal time analysis, look at the results, then study the alternatives listed below and circle those which most apply to you. As a precaution, it might be advisable to check your views with your subordinates and with your boss, in case your perception of yourself differs from theirs: indeed, as your 'customers', they may well be better placed to make judgements about your frailty than you are, particularly if you're inclined (as most human beings are) to become defensive when engaging in self-analysis. Once you've got some agreement about the likely causes of your time management difficulties, however, it is much easier to know where to concentrate your efforts to improve.

Issue 1: Too much to read
In the 1980s there was much talk among office management intellectuals about a phenomenon called 'the paperless office'. From the vantage point of the 1990s, there is no evidence whatsoever that the paperless office is on its way. It's not even peeping over the horizon. The causes are threefold:

- Computer systems generate lots of print-out.
- The ubiquitous photocopier encourages documents to be reproduced for large distribution lists, because the production of copies is itself so painless.
- Fax machines spew out letters, memos, circulars and reports, the immediacy of the fax process promoting a quite false belief in the urgency and importance of whatever is being transmitted.

Possible Solutions and Remedies

1. Get someone else to scrutinize your incoming mail before you get it, discard all items not critical to your key tasks, and distribute items which can be dealt with by others.
2. Talk to the information-systems people to ensure that the computer print-out they send you is the computer print-out you want, rather than the computer print-out they want you to have. After all, you are their customer, not the other way round.
3. If necessary, get yourself taken off the print-out distribution list altogether.
4. Maybe it would be better if one of your staff received the print-out, scrutinized it, and reported to you 'by exception', i.e., took account of only those items where there is a significant deviation from the norm and where, therefore, some action could be imminent.
5. Take yourself off unwanted distribution lists by stopping the material at source.
6. Think more carefully about distribution for your own material. Who really needs it? Am I sending this to anybody because I'm trying to impress them rather than because they actually want it? (If you're into networking, of course, then trying to impress people is perfectly OK and you wouldn't delete

someone's name from your circulation list if impressing them were the sole reason for sending them something.)

7. Learn something of the skills of rapid reading. First you may have to put aside some misconceptions about the process of reading. For example, it is commonly believed that faster reading generates lower concentration, when precisely the opposite is true: the faster we go, the higher our concentration has to be. A slow reader is more likely to become bored and vulnerable to distractions. Then, secondly, the basis of speed reading involves classifying whatever you have to read so that you choose the appropriate reading technique:

- **Study Reading** is relevant when the material is difficult and 100 per cent comprehension is required (e.g., the fine print of legal documents). The approach here *is* necessarily slow, with reading and rereading, making notes, and giving full consideration to the various meanings and implications of the material.
- **Slow Reading** makes sense if you're going through a novel, perhaps, but has little application in a business context. Even when you're reading a novel, you don't normally study every word.
- **Rapid Reading** implies average speeds of between 300 and 800 words per minute, with an acceptable level of comprehension. The method requires words to be 'batched' into groups so that you pick up the sense rather than the precise meaning. You can train your eyes to go down the centre of the page of text, reading some words on each line and only moving to the left and right if the message looks significant.
- **Skimming** allows the eyes to move quickly down *and*

across the page, not reading every group of words nor even every line. This technique should be used when a general outline or overview of the material is required: you can achieve speeds of between 1000 and 2000 words per minute by simply paying attention to headings, sub-headings, opening and closing sentences/paragraphs, and key words or sentences. If you have other people who produce written material on your behalf (in draft form, perhaps), you can ask them to identify critical episodes of the text in advance, with the aid of underlining, highlighter pens, and so forth.

- **Previewing** is similar to skimming, but here we are looking for specific information to help us decide whether it is actually necessary to read the material at all. We can look at the document's title, contents page, date, distribution list, maps/diagrams/pictures, chapter headings, recommendations (if any), and a sample of paragraphs (especially the first and last sentences). If the document is a report already supplied with a Management Summary, then our task is typically made much easier.

Issue 2: Inadequate information
Paradoxically, you can be inundated with paper and yet simultaneously find yourself deprived of the information you *really* need.

Possible Solutions and Remedies
1. Think about where or how you could get the information you *really* need. Then talk to the potential suppliers (often inside your organization) who could give it to you. Negotiating with one of these suppliers may be easier than you think, especially as internal service providers in organizations are nowadays

more switched on to the concept of supplying the requirements of their 'customers'. Also you may be able to suggest a trade-off, in which information you don't need is stopped, and the recourses allocated instead to something that you would genuinely value.

2. If the information you *really* need is already being prepared but is going to someone else (e.g., your boss) and you never see it, then put up a case for being added to the circulation (or preferably the distribution) list.

3. If the information you *really* need is held by your staff, set up a reporting system to ensure that it reaches you in a timely and user-friendly basis.

4. Check with others who do a similar job to yours: would they also like the information that you think you *really* need? If so, devise some collective lobbying to make sure you start to get it – group action is almost always more productive than the pressure from a lonely individual. If your colleagues don't agree with you about the necessity for the information you have in mind, then you may be forced to re-examine your own priorities.

Issue 3: Too many crises

Arguably, **every crisis is an indictment of the manager and the organization which employs him.** And yet the crises keep on coming: why?

• Partly it's because every crisis is stimulating, exciting, adrenalin-packed, and gives the crisis manager a completely false sense of achievement.

• Some crises, let's face it, are deliberately manufactured in order to give bored managers something to do. If that seems absurd, think about the international confrontations which have been engineered by political leaders to divert attention from disaffection at home.

- We can't predict everything and so some crises are bound to take us by surprise. And even if a crisis has been predicted, we may think that the probability of its occurrence is so remote that it would not be cost-effective to cater for it; or that the damage it will do cannot be sufficient to justify a pre-emptive strike.

- Some managers act as if it is *only* the existence of crises which justifies their existence: if the crises disappeared, then so would their jobs. These managers, therefore, have no desire to be proactive because they see the elimination of crises as directly opposed to their own best (survival) interests.

- Spending time on crises means that less time is available for predicting, anticipating, preventing and minimizing the crises of tomorrow. Small wonder that some people find crisis management so appealing: it's the 'comfort zone' of the known and familiar, contrasted with the frightening void of the unknown.

Having said all this, and having made every allowance for differences of judgement about whether this or that crisis could (and should) have been predicted, there is undoubtedly room for more prevention and control.

Possible Solutions and Remedies

1. Once a critical situation has been resolved, we should undertake a systematic future-crisis-prevention analysis, to establish whether it would be cost-effective to establish systems for making sure that the same crisis does not recur. To make this judgement, we need answers to these questions:

- What is the probability that a similar crisis will happen again?
- What is the most damage that a similar crisis could cause to us and to the organization?
- If the probability of a recurrence is sufficiently high, and the repercussions sufficiently awe-inspiring, then what can we do to prevent it, or to mitigate its impact?

2. When making plans for the future, employ a Devil's Advocate to tell you what can go wrong – then tie up the loose ends. Brainstorming can be helpful here, by getting a group together to address the question, 'In how many ways can these plans fail?'
3. Delegate the process of crisis-management to people beneath you (who probably caused the crisis anyway) on the grounds that they are better equipped to handle operational and day-to-day issues of that kind. The higher you go in the managerial hierarchy, the more you need to distance yourself from anything other than the really big crises (like the threat to poison large quantities of your company's products).
4. Learn to back off from excessive hands-on involvement in (and even provocation of) every crisis you encounter. There's just as much satisfaction and excitement to be gained from managing proactively as from managing reactively: and we are supposed to be moving towards a 'right first time' scenario.

Issue 4: Poor delegation

It is astonishing to see the number of managers who busy themselves with activities which could be handled by their own subordinates. Why they do this, why they don't delegate, and what to do about it, are themes addressed in Chapter Seven.

Issue 5: Too many telephone calls

It is often claimed that one of the easiest ways of gaining spoken access to someone is to phone them, always provided you have their direct-line number, because nobody can resist answering the phone, even if they're in the middle of a meeting, a selection interview, a complex negotiation scenario or a blazing row. So, telephone calls are a frequent (and annoying) source of interruptions in themselves, but the situation is made worse by the long-winded rigmarole in which incoming callers indulge before they get to the point. Chapter Four contains many hints and guidelines on preventing unwanted phone calls and restricting their duration to acceptable limits.

Issue 6: Too many face-to-face interruptions

When you're working in an open-plan office you may consider yourself to be uniquely vulnerable to interruptions from occasional visitors, whose opening gambit is typically some phrase like 'Have you got a minute?' **Never has the word 'minute' been more abused:** if you were to say, 'Yes, I have a maximum of sixty seconds,' they would gaze at you uncomprehending because, of course, they were speaking metaphorically rather than literally. At least, that's what they would say if you challenged them: what they really want to do, when they begin with 'Have you got a minute?' is to gain your attention. In fact you will have been a victim of confidence-trickery because the matter they want to discuss will *not* take a mere 60 seconds.

Further, even if the first topic on the visitor's agenda can be put to bed inside the advertised time-span, something else will be raised. This second item will be far more problematic and will be the real reason for the interruption. It is an example of what GPs call the

33

'presenting problem' scenario: the patient opens with some triviality, but eventually (just when they're on the point of leaving), they say something like 'Oh, by the way, Doctor, while I was here I thought I might ask you about . . .'

As we shall see when we approach the topic of interruption-management in greater depth, the damage caused to your time management by any given interruption is always **twice as long as the actual duration of the interruption itself**. This is because, if the interruption lasts for five minutes, it will take you a further five minutes to reorientate your concentration back to what you were doing before. Sometimes the adjustment process proves impossible, if the visitor's topic was sufficiently juicy, frightening, threatening or rewarding. In extreme cases, you may yourself be inspired to go and interrupt others, and so a cascade of time-wasting is formed.

Solutions and remedies for face-to-face interruptions are proposed in Chapter Four. This will be undoubtedly one of the most important chapters in the whole book. It fleshes out the idea, proposed in Chapter Two, that an unrestricted 'open door' policy is disastrous, and suggests some devices which will enable you to be both accessible but also help you get some value-added work done.

Issue 7: Meetings

Generally speaking, we can distinguish here between your own meetings, which are well-managed, well-organized and productive; or the meetings held by others, which are poorly-led, badly run and a scandalous waste of time. Once we've got that distinction clearly understood, then we can make progress.

Quite typically a middle manager may spend more

than half his time each week at a succession of meetings. And if the definition of 'meeting' is extended to include any discussion between two or more people that is designed to achieve an objective, we can them embrace one-to-one interviews (selection, appraisal, discipline) and visits to (actual or prospective) customers: incorporating the time devoted to such gatherings will raise the proportion of meeting-attendance to something like two-thirds or even three-quarters.

One might suppose that this constantly recurring *modus operandi* would eventually generate a corpus of experience and professionalism in the preparation for and conduct of meetings, but there seems to be little evidence for it.

As with the issues of face-to-face and telephone interruptions, this book contains a separate chapter about meetings, offering guidance to formally-appointed chairmen, informally-selected discussion leaders, and also to the people attending meetings and discussions (willingly or otherwise): how can they all manage the time more productively and go away from their meeting feeling satisfied, even elated, rather than frustrated, angry and inadequate?

Issue 8: Overambition

One difficulty faced by some people is that they constantly misjudge the time it will take to complete something. As a result, they commit themselves to too much (it's usually that way rather than trying to do too little), and some projects, objectives and activities get left behind, with a consequential failure to meet critical deadlines.

Possible Solutions and Remedies
1. Learn from your mistakes. Review some particularly

horrendous situation where the discrepancy between your estimated time for completion and the actual time taken was very noticeable. Why did the discrepancy arise? Was there some component part of the task which took much longer than expected? If so, did it take longer because it genuinely needed more time, or because you didn't want to do it for some reason and therefore kept putting it to one side? If it genuinely required more time, you will know what to do in future when quoting deadlines. If the delay arose because of your feelings about the task (or some part of it), there may be scope for overcoming your fears, doubts or anxieties through training. If resources can be found you may be able to delegate it to someone for whom the task holds no terrors.

2. Before committing yourself to deadlines, produce a critical path (if only for yourself) showing each phase in the task completion process, with a defensible time estimate for each. If you allow for an element of slippage – say, 10 per cent – then your overall judgements about duration will be far more accurate.

3. Discuss your 'first-guess' time estimates with a colleague more experienced than yourself before going public with any promises. It may well be that contributions from an independent observer will remind you of potential obstacles and hazards that you should have included in your planning.

Issue 9: Procrastination
In our experience, many managers think they are managing their time effectively if they use a 'Things To Do' list. Some organizations have produced notepads with the words 'Things To Do' at the top of each page and the numbers 1 to 20 down the left-hand side: a fact which

creates enormous pressure to find 20 things to do. However, producing a list of things to do is only the start. Looking at the list, you then have to decide which things to do first, and this is where the system breaks down because many people – weak and fallible as they are – select top priority items against the following criteria:

- Those activities which will bring 'quick wins' for little effort.
- Those activities which the manager finds more enjoyable, or easier, or within his current 'comfort zone'.

Conversely, tasks which look forbidding – because they involve intellectual challenge, or possible confrontations with others, or extended effort before completion – will be postponed, sometimes for ever. Almost certainly this means that any projects which require thinking will be put to one side, in accordance with Henry Ford's observation that 'Thinking is the hardest work there is, and that's why so few managers engage in it.' Every single example of such procrastinating will be entirely justified in the manager's mind, of course, by the skilful exercise of intellectual legerdemain and self-justifying rationalization: but nonetheless it constitutes defensive evasion of the worst kind.

Possible Solutions and Remedies

1. The first and most obvious suggestion involves the disciplined use of a priority system which will be examined in greater depth as part of Chapter Four:

- **Quadrant A: Work which is both Important and Urgent.**
  Items allocated to this slot will be dealt with *quickly*

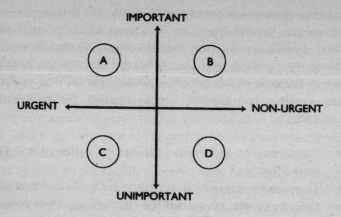

(i.e., today, or even this morning) and will be allocated a *generous time-slot* because of their significance.

- **Quadrant B: Work which is Important but Non-Urgent.**
  The preparation of proactive strategies for adding value – through Performance Improvement and Change Management – fits broadly into this category. One important danger of classifying something as Non-Urgent, however, is that it may be put to one side, with the result that it suddenly becomes very Urgent indeed as a forgotten deadline looms up out of the mist like a hazardous iceberg. Some time should always be scheduled for Quadrant B activities so that they are pushed forward: by delegating investigative activities to your staff, by setting up a project team, by approaching others (consultants, colleagues in other organizations, professional bodies, your network contacts) for advice and input, or simply by sketching out a few thoughts for yourself.
- **Quadrant C: Work which is Urgent but Unimportant.**
  The fact that something is important to somebody

else does not automatically mean that it is important to you: much depends on how significant that somebody else is, in your eyes. So if a subordinate wants immediate compassionate leave, that is clearly very important to him, but much less so to you; on the other hand, customer complaints warrant being classified as both Urgent and Important, since customers themselves deserve the highest priority. Tasks in Quadrant C, therefore, should be allocated small time-slots and may even be delegated to others as a matter of routine.

- **Quadrant D: Work which is neither Urgent nor Important.**
  The waste-paper bin is the proper place for tasks coming into this category. Alternatively, your rapid-reading skills can be useful in helping you to extract the occasional nugget of useful information from a mass of trivia.

2. Constant use of these questions, applied to everything that is put in front of you:

- Does this task fit closely with my personal value-added mission for the organization?
- Does it add value?
- If it doesn't, can I delegate it, or get rid of it altogether?
- What will happen if I don't do it at all?

Issue 10: Poor organization
It becomes very difficult for you to manage your time properly if you're working in an environment of permanent ambiguity, confusion and conflict. In the typical organization of the 1990s, some ambiguity is virtually inevitable, as jobs form and re-form themselves around

changing business needs, but if there is nothing but ambiguity then you have nothing firm to stand on. Ambiguity can be found when hierarchical relationships are unclear; when you have more than one boss (a particular issue in matrix or project-team structures); when you are competing directly with others for resources; when your authority limits are vague and imprecise; and when the job is actually too big to be done properly by a single human being. Confusion and uncertainty are bound to exist if you are supposed to manage effectively in a context where the organization's goals and strategies are concealed from you (or where, perhaps, they don't exist). In scenarios like that, your priorities must simply be a matter for personal choice, or a reflection of what you imagine the organization wants from you – but you could be devastatingly wrong.

Possible Solutions and Remedies

1. Obtain some guidance or clarification from your boss about his priorities, because that will help you determine where your time should be allocated.
2. If your boss is as much in the dark as you are, then together you should work out some defensible initiatives, based on whatever information you do have available: these initiatives can be presented to and discussed with whoever is next up the hierarchical line.
3. Keep going up the hierarchy until you do get some feedback.
4. Create your own value-added initiatives and priorities, but make sure you tell everyone what you're doing, so that if anybody significant wants to object they have the opportunity to do so.
5. If you are required to undertake activities for more than one person (e.g., in a project-based or matrix

structure), and this creates conflicts of priorities which you find impossible to manage, then try to get your respective 'bosses' to talk to each other so that *they* agree your priorities for you. This is not a particularly good strategy from your point of view, however, as it will create extra work for these 'bosses' and will make you look ineffectual: far better to manage the situation within your own resources, by working smarter, by delegating some of the conflicting activities, or by temporarily dispensing with other (postponable) tasks.

Issue 11: Unclear objectives

'If you don't know where you're going, how will you know when you get there?' is a cliché in textbooks about managing by objectives. The fact that it is a cliché does not automatically make it untrue: we believe that a value-added mission statement, linked with up to six key tasks (or key results areas) which together will account for about 80 per cent of your value-added effectiveness, is an essential prelude to the production of meaningful objectives. However, some objectives are better than others, and a few are little more than a pious hope, because of the vague and imprecise way they are written ('My objective is to get on better with the people I work with'). In our judgement, the only objectives worth having are those which meet the 'TRAMPS' criteria:

- **Time-bounded:** there is a definite deadline for delivering the result.
- **Result-oriented:** the objective focuses on one of your key (value-added) result areas, rather than a 'mere' efficiency input. Objectives to do with getting to work on time, for example, scarcely represent added-value in themselves.

- **Attainable:** you have to believe there is a chance of attaining your goal, otherwise it's likely that you'll give up before you begin.
- **Measurable:** the achievement of the result should be signalled by the attainment of a quantified target point (the deadline may itself be a significant part of the measurable component for the objective).
- **Precise:** a single-minded concentration on a readily-definable area of your value-added job performance and role.
- **Stretching:** attainment of the objective is going to force you to put out some extra effort, in terms of time disciplines, learning, training, and so forth.

Possible Solutions and Remedies

It sounds simple to advise that if you haven't any objectives, or you have some objectives but they don't meet the 'TRAMPS' criteria, then you go out and get some. Ask your boss (or your 'customers') for some proper objectives, seek more precision in the objectives you've already got, and produce some suggestions of your own if your overtures with your boss don't produce results. Some managers have been known to tell us that they are quite happy to operate without clear objectives, because this means that their performance can never be criticized (since nobody knew what they were supposed to be doing anyway). In reality quite the opposite is true, and such managers are guilty of the worst kind of defeatist defensiveness. By not having objectives they lay themselves open to adverse feedback on a broad front, on the grounds that they should have known what their objectives and priorities were; the absence of objectives also means that good performance and achievements are less likely to be recognized; and if you have no objectives, it's impossible to make sensible judgements about priorities when time conflicts occur.

With some jobs, objective-setting is relatively straight-forward. It's not difficult to specify 'TRAMPS'-led performance criteria for production, sales and marketing positions. With other organizational roles, and even with parts of the roles for managers in production, sales and marketing, the process is more problematic because of the difficulty of quantifying that which does not easily lend itself to quantification. It could certainly be a mistake to assume that things are important simply because they are measurable, yet what seems to happen when the objective-setting mentality takes over is that managers 'forget' those key tasks where quantified objectives are difficult to specify, and concentrate instead on others where, say, percentage improvements make plausible sense.

To overcome the issues surrounding the production of 'TRAMPS' objectives for such key tasks as, say, self-development or the maintenance of smooth working relationships with colleagues, we can make one positive suggestion. It's pointless to commit yourself to objectives like spending at least 10 per cent of your time on self-development, or establishing co-operative links with your fellow managers: both of these supposed objectives are imprecise, ambiguous and unquantifiable. The only way forward, in our view, is to produce objectives to do with *activities* leading to *results* whose achievement is conditional upon effective performance in the behavioural dimension being addressed. Thus, if teamwork is the issue, you could specify an objective concerned with managing a project group or working party, the results of whose activities would be measurable, specific and precise; the attainment of the result would in turn depend upon your interpersonal and leadership skills. The development of these skills would be at least as significant as the tangible product of the project team, and so the 'end' would be evidence of the 'means', as it were.

Issue 12: Personal disorganization

There's no doubt about it: if your workstation is a nightmare of papers, letters, old coffee cups, paperclips, print-out, newspapers, magazines and sandwich wrappers, then your efficiency is low and your effectiveness even lower. Searching through piles of papers not only wastes valuable time, it also means, inevitably, that some pieces of paper will get lost or mixed up with other things. Nor does a cluttered, confusing workstation look good to others. Your boss probably won't be impressed (unless he/she operates the same way!) and you'll be setting an example of *apparently* incompetent fire-fighting to your subordinates. We say 'apparently' because there are some managers who, when challenged about the shambles in which they work, will say 'I know where everything is' and will even seek to prove it to you. Frankly, we disbelieve such claims and regard them as nothing more than an ego-defence from people who've never tried to be efficient and therefore don't know what they're missing. Such people often sneer about personal efficiency, too, as if it were nothing more than the trademark of the administrative nit-picker, instead of being a necessary prelude to adding value.

Possible Solutions and Remedies

Although some managers appear to think that 'an empty desk indicates an empty mind', and therefore clutter up their desks in order to appear frantically busy, we prefer to subscribe to the belief that 'an empty desk indicates a tidy mind'. So you have to start by clearing your desk: emptying it of magazines, phone messages, unanswered correspondence, unfinished reports, futile memos, old pages of print-out and Post-It notes stuck on to all available surfaces. All this mess has to be cleaned up.

Next, you announce to all and sundry that you're not in to callers or visitors: all your colleagues and sources of interruption have to imagine that you're on holiday or off sick. After that you take four boxes and mark them 'Background reading', 'Junk mail', 'Routine' and 'Priority'. Everything from your desk goes into one of these boxes: low priority items go into the box marked 'Routine', bearing in mind that the definition of high priority, for inclusion in the 'Priority' box, means anything which has to be actioned within three working days. Clearing your desk so that everything is put into one of these boxes shouldn't take more than 30 minutes; if it does, it will be because you've stopped to read something or even to think about it.

Once everything is allocated into the four boxes, you can take the 'Priority' box and deal with everything in it, one item at a time. Some can be disposed of quickly, while others may take an hour or so. Once the 'Priority' box is empty, you can turn to the 'Routine' items and get rid of them even more quickly. 'Junk mail' can usually be jettisoned; 'Background reading' needs to be scanned, to see if there's anything worth copying or tearing out (or, even better, tearing up), but it can then be thrown away or passed on to someone else. If the magazine is one you never asked for and don't find relevant, attack the source in an effort to stop it from reaching you in the first place.

There is enormous psychological advantage in emptying your desk, even if the suddenly-acquired space only represents an illusion so far as value-added work is concerned. Of course, if you've emptied your desk once, you have to keep it up, but at least you've proved that you can do it.

Issue 13: Socializing

Too many casual conversations, on non-work topics, are always going to get in the way of getting anything done. Clearly there is a case for *some* socializing: part of it counts as networking, some of it oils the wheels of your job, and some of it represents a short-term relief from pressure. What we mean here, however, is the kind of situation where a colleague arrives at your desk, carrying a fresh cup of coffee, a happy smile on his face, saying 'Hallo, Bob, how are you?' or 'Here, have you heard about June and Jim?' Sometimes enthusiastically, other times less so, you put aside whatever you were doing and prepare to engage in aimless activity or listen to some juicy gossip. Better still, you are invited to discuss something that your visitor saw on last night's television and which (he hopes) you saw as well.

Possible Solutions and Remedies

If you develop a reputation for welcoming these pointless interruptions from people who seemingly have little to do (actually they probably have lots to do but their time management is even worse than yours), then the number of such interruptions will go on rising. How do you develop such a reputation? By welcoming the first pointless interruption, of course, and then the second, until it becomes a habit. So turning back the tide, if you're already known to be a sociable character, is going to be difficult: it's much easier to avoid acquiring the reputation in the first place.

A later chapter will deal in more depth with some techniques for preventing and controlling interruptions. If you're just starting out, however, and you don't want to fall into the socializing trap, you may be able to locate your workstation so that you don't automatically engage eye contact with would-be interrupters. You certainly don't have an empty chair on the other side of your desk – a permanent signal that you welcome occasional visitors – and your body language should give some clues about your attitude whenever confronted with gratuitous interruptions. You don't smile, you react slowly to the interruption, you avoid looking at the visitor, you glance at your watch, you tap your fingers on the desk. Of course, you can also say things like 'Sorry, Bill, I haven't time to talk now', reinforced by the claimed need to finish a report by 11 o'clock, if you wish. Oddly enough, too, if someone begins a conversation by asking whether you saw *World in Action* last night, your affirmative reply (whether you did or not) will often encourage them to discuss the programme with you: it is typically preferable to talk in negative terms. Not only did you not see it, but also you're not interested. They will soon go elsewhere in search of someone who knows what your interrupter is talking about, because he too is a couch potato.

All of these ploys, and more, are equally available to the manager who suddenly realizes why his time is being wasted and decides to do something about his reputation for being a soft social touch. It will be harder work because it must take some time before regular interrupters get the message. Such people may have to be spoken to quite directly and even brutally before they realize that you mean it. Even then they will put you to the test from time to time. You must be ever-watchful, ever-vigilant: one slip will be enough to cause your previous image to be resurrected and then you have to start all over again.

And Finally

These 13 issues don't represent a comprehensive list of time bandits, but they are undoubtedly the most common. If you apply some of the solutions and remedies applicable to your symptoms, then you will release time presently dissipated so that it can be put to more productive (and value-added) use. Training of others (especially your subordinates), the systematic use of delegation, a clearer sense of performance-improvement priorities, the prevention and control of interruptions, effective management of the boss, greater discipline and self-control in selecting (and rejecting) activities – all of these will help you powerfully to gain some ascendancy over this most unforgiving and relentless resource. Most of all, you must clarify your own role, your purpose (i.e., your job 'mission' expressed in value-added language), your key tasks and your objectives: only then can judgements about priorities be made sensibly, founded on the achievement of results rather than simply the selection of enjoyable, interesting and 'comfort-zone' things.

CHAPTER 4

Dealing With Interruptions

ORGANIZING YOUR TIME

Time management has to be attacked from two directions simultaneously:

1. You need to have **defensible work priorities and objectives** so that you have a rationale for allocating your time to one activity rather than another.
2. You need to establish a **routine** for coping with the things you have to do but which don't add value.

WORK PRIORITIES AND OBJECTIVES

We've already made the point about developing a succinct, one-sentence **value-added mission statement** showing how you contribute to your organization. This statement should be no more than six words (ten at the most), should be free job-description-speak, and should begin with an upward-sounding verb.

From this mission statement will stem up to six **key tasks** or **key result areas**: those parts of your job which account for 80 per cent of your value-added contribution but which, at present, take up only 20 per cent of your time.

This is fine so far as your job is concerned. But what about *you* as a person? If you're ambitious (and even if you're not), it's wise to distinguish between the objectives formally associated with your role, and your *personal* objectives (e.g., for career advancement, for job satisfaction, for job security, for a sense of achievement and fulfilment). Certainly if you want to get promoted, then part of your time must be devoted to networking and image-building with those people (normally your seniors) who have it in their power to help you achieve your (personal) goal. To some extent your promotability stems from the degree to which you are seen to add value in the organization, but most authorities agree that there are equally vital dimensions concerned with interpersonal acceptance and simply getting yourself known.

You must check out your mission statement and your key tasks with those responsible for assessing your performance. If you can secure some agreement from your boss about what you have to do in order to add value, then this can be valuable in turning away irrelevant tasks which other people (including, sometimes, your boss!) may try to impose on you. And if you can't turn them away, at least your mission statement and key tasks will be invaluable in helping you to judge priorities on a sensible basis. Always remember, however, that you have some *personal* objectives too, and they may require you to ingratiate yourself with somebody who wants you to do something unconnected to your central role in the organization. If the Managing Director asks you to produce some visual aids for his major presentation to the shareholders, it could be career-limiting to decline on the grounds that your job is more concerned with marketing innovation and planning.

ESTABLISHING A ROUTINE

Routines can be a jailer as well as a liberator. A routine is a jailer if it generates such well-worn and comfortable habits that life (and your work) becomes boring, your brain atrophies, your reactions become stereotyped, and your colleagues know precisely what to expect from you.

Routine is a liberator if it means that you become organized so that you can devote more time to the challenging, the original, the innovative, the path-finding, the management of change. Routine becomes your salvation when it releases you from the mundane and, better still, when it enables others to organize themselves around you, leaving you to get on with your *real* work.

The Use of Secretaries
If you're powerful enough to have a secretary, then you're probably not reading this book: get your secretary to read it for you and distil the points relevant to you.

If you don't have a secretary but you do have subordinates, you may be able to organize one of those subordinates to intercept phone calls, to prioritize your mail, and to help protect you from unplanned and unwanted interruptions.

If you don't have a secretary and you don't have any subordinates either, then you must perform the secretary's role yourself.

The following paragraphs, therefore, apply to your secretary, or to your subordinates, or to you, according to taste (and the availability of resources).

If you come to work each day and find your in-tray put together in a higgledy-piggledy fashion, the contents thrown on to your desk more or less according to the chronological sequence of their arrival, then you have a training problem. Your secretary must be instructed to arrange your work to take account of your (and the organization's) priorities.

There is only one systematic way for sensibly determining priorities, and this involves looking at tasks in terms of their **Urgency** and their **Importance**.

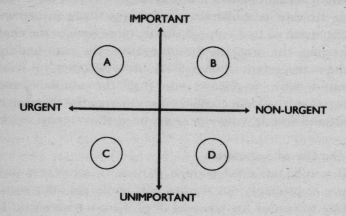

Quadrant (A) is Work which is both Important and Urgent. 'Urgent' means that you must do it today, and 'Important' means that doing it will add value, or not doing it will result in a serious loss of value (so you have to do whatever it is as part of a damage limitation exercise). Tasks in quadrant (A) will normally be given a generous time-slot, reflecting their significance.

Quadrant (B) is Work which is Important but not Urgent. Things which will add value but which don't have a tight deadline can be put in this quadrant. You can start things moving on the quadrant (B) items today (for example, by asking a subordinate to do some information-gathering on your behalf, or by planning a critical path leading to completion of a project) but a substantial allocation of time can be left until later: perhaps to a day or a week when you can predict you'll have less fire-fighting to do or fewer tight deadlines to meet. Most jobs have a cyclical character about them, i.e., there will be times of the day, or days of the week, or weeks in the month, when you can legitimately expect that you will be rushed off your feet, and other periods when you can plan on the basis of having relatively little day-to-day work. These are the periods when quadrant (B) activity can be scheduled. It is dangerous to neglect or forget about quadrant (B) tasks, because they are often the relatively long-term ideas which need some foresight and planning before they lead to fruition, and they are the things where the generous investment of time produces a correspondingly significant pay-off in terms of added value. It is also dangerous to put quadrant (B) tasks to one side for too long. You may then find that suddenly they've crept up on you and they're now in quadrant (A), with a deadline of next week or even tomorrow, so you now have no time to complete the assignment properly. What is worse is a situation where you deliberately put a quadrant (B) job on one side, thinking you'll do it in the final working days before the deadline, only to find as those days approach that they're already half-full with other quadrant (A) activities. Sod's Law ('If anything can go wrong, it will') also dictates that it is in these final days that you become ill and so the important deadline is missed altogether. It will be no excuse to say that you had influenza just before the deadline, if the task had been given to you six months earlier: you should have planned for the possibility of being ill!

Quadrant (C) is Work which is Urgent but not Important. It has to be dealt with today, but deserves only a small time-slot because it is not significant seen against your value-added mission. Tasks in quadrant (C) lend themselves readily to being delegated, being passed back whence they came (on the grounds that the person giving you the task should have handled it himself), being disposed of quickly through your own instant decision, or even being thrown into the waste-bin.

Quadrant (D) refers to Work which is neither Urgent nor Important. Reading journals and magazines which have arrived on your desk without you asking for them; looking at reports whose authors have put you on their distribution list even if the subject matter is irrelevant to you; discussing arrangements for the Christmas decorations – in August. Why waste time at all on these kinds of things? Most of them can safely be discarded and thrown in the bin, quickly scanned and passed to someone else, or delegated to others as a matter of routine.

If you look at the **Urgency/Importance** matrix, and start to think that virtually everything you have to do is in quadrant (A), this means that you must simply draw an **Urgency/Importance** matrix *inside quadrant (A).* Even if everything on your plate is both Urgent and Important, you cannot physically do more than one thing at a time. If you try, you will rapidly go insane, so you cannot avoid having to make choices: in other words, you have to select priority tasks from among all the high-priority tasks.

Another point worth making concerns the definition of 'Important'. What is important to someone else isn't necessarily important to you. Much depends on the importance of that someone else. If your Chief Executive asks you to do something, it would normally be wise to view that task as Important (and probably Urgent), simply because of the significance of the person who's giving you the job. Equally, if one of your 'customers' rings up with a complaint, it would be sensible to put the resolution of that complaint in quadrant (A), not necessarily because of the world-shaking nature of the complaint itself (indeed, it may be trivial), but rather because of the pedestal on which we have nowadays placed 'customers' (whether internal or external). So classifying something as 'Important' depends on:

- The value-added significance of the task; or
- The potential damage which could be caused if the task is not performed or is done badly; or
- The significance (to you) of the person giving you the task.

You may ask: what happens if I have things given to me, more or less simultaneously, by my Chief Executive *and* by one of my 'customers'? How do I decide which to do first? In this book we can offer no definite answer to this question. We know what the answer should be in an ideal world, because your Chief Executive should be delighted to learn that you have given preference to resolving a 'customer' complaint. However, we also know that the world is very far from being ideal, and you may find that despite all the protestations about 'The Customer is King', your Chief Executive expects privileged treatment. If you wish to continue in paid employment, and want to score highly in perceived effectiveness so far as your Chief Executive is concerned, it could be career-limiting to ignore such political realities.

In short, when you are contemplating the pile of things on your desk, or looking at your long list of 'Things To Do', these are the questions to ask:

1. *Will it add value?* Is this activity relevant to my added-value mission for the organization? Is it going to contribute to my real and perceived effectiveness? Does it come under the umbrella of Performance Improvement and/or Change Management, i.e., the parts of my role which are concerned with adding value?

2. *Where has this task come from?* Who has given it to me (assuming it is not self-initiated)? You may know that the task is important for the person who has passed it to you, but is that person important to you? Can the task be left without serious interpersonal repercussions, in other words?

3. *What will happen if I don't do it?* Must I give it high priority if only for damage-limitation purposes? Will anyone notice if I don't do it? (It's a continual source of surprise for us when we uncover tasks and routines in organizations which are a legacy of the past and continue to be performed despite the fact that they serve no useful purpose.)

4. *Can it be delegated?* When in doubt, delegate. If you can't get rid of the whole thing, then delegate part of it. If you don't have staff, then can you persuade someone else to do it, not only now but also in the future?

5. *Can I spend less time on it?* If the task comes into the arena of Maintenance, and therefore does not add value, can I focus more clearly on only those aspects which genuinely matter, rather than poking about with information which is 'interesting'? Can I read faster? Can I get the information presented to me in a more 'user-friendly' way so that, for example, I don't have to hunt among pages of statistics in order to find the figures I want?

If you should ask these questions about your own work, and use the **Urgency/Importance** system for classifying your own priorities, then your secretary could do so as well. Obviously you and your secretary may differ about the quadrant into which a given task (memo, letter, phone message) should be fitted, and sometimes there are genuine differences of judgement involved, but the more you work together the closer your respective evaluations are likely to become. Anything is better than coming to work and finding that your mail is simply thrown on to your desk in reverse chronological order, with no attempt at sorting, prioritizing or even the linking of connected items.

Quite often things will get to you when they belong properly to someone else – perhaps one of your staff or a colleague, or even your boss. A properly-trained secretary can immediately divert such tasks to the person in question, without them ever reaching you. The beauty of this arrangement is that once it's in place, time is saved for you not only on the day it starts, but on all subsequent days. Even better is if you can ensure that the originators of such tasks contact the appropriate person directly in the first place instead of writing to you. Not only is your time saved as a result, but the originators will get a quicker – and, let's face it, a more competent – response because the person they approach is the one who knows more about the situation, how it arose and how it can be resolved. This is especially true if the originator happens to be a 'customer', and the task concerns a complaint. Writing to the manager may seem the obvious thing to do (and sometimes it is very effective), but if an organization is genuinely dedicated to customer service then writing to the person who actually deals with your business should prove quicker and ultimately more satisfying.

If secretaries are being properly used as secretaries, then they should be answering routine mail themselves. Initially this means drafting material for you to approve and sign, but ultimately it suggests that they send off their own letters.

Your time becomes more effective if you do everything you can to help secretaries (and subordinates generally) to plan their working routines. A meeting at the start of the day can work wonders – to review your diary, your meetings and your appointments, and to agree action plans for the most Important and Urgent matters needing attention. People don't like being treated like human yo-yos, being called in to be given one thing to do and then, a few moments later, being called in yet again for something else: so plan your work allocation system so that everyone is given, at one go, all the things they can be doing on your behalf. This allocation routine should preferably take place at the beginning of the day, too, rather than towards the end (when it will mean that people suffer from enforced idleness during the day but have to stay late to complete your last-minute assignments).

It makes sense, too, to review progress with your secretary and other key staff at the end of the day, to ensure that everything urgent has been done and that unforeseen obstacles have been surmounted.

Restricting Access to Yourself

Rigid adherence to the chain of command becomes something of an academic and bureaucratic exercise these days, with the emergence of flattened, informal hierarchies and the fashion for 'empowerment'. However, it is still legitimate to ask whether there is any point in having a hierarchy at all, if people are allowed to by-pass it with impunity. We've already argued that an unrestricted 'open door' policy is disastrous for anyone who takes time management seriously, so saying 'No' to people who ask to see you becomes perfectly acceptable.

By-passing the chain of command produces gratuitous additions to your workload. Also, it undermines the status and power of the persons by-passed, and it generates role conflict for the people who do the by-passing because they now regard themselves as having two bosses.

Whatever your job, you should be able to draw up a list of (a) all those people who have unlimited access to you, (b) all those for whom your time is available on a restricted or negotiable basis, and (c) the people you should avoid altogether. The list might look like this:

A	UNRESTRICTED
B	RESTRICTED
C	AVOID

It's surprising how few individuals can earn the right to occupy your category A (Unrestricted): your 'customers', perhaps, if you're consciously following a customer-care programme and giving them the priority they deserve, but even then there will be some 'customers' who are more important than others (because they are more senior, or they spend more with you) and who will therefore get your personal attention rather than redirection to one of your colleagues. Obviously your Managing Director, Chief Executive, and other very powerful people will be in category A so far as you're concerned: to do otherwise could deal a fatal blow to your perceived effectiveness.

An Interesting Question: if you were faced with simultaneous demands on your time from your Managing Director and a customer, who should be given priority? Certainly customers are unlikely to be sympathetic if they find out that their demands have been downgraded, figuratively speaking, by the internal requirements of the organizations. On the other hand, it's our experience that there aren't many organizations where, if you give preference to a customer, you will subsequently receive a bouquet from the Managing Director whose requirements have been pushed down to second place. We know what the correct answer is (customers should always have precedence), but once again you have to be attentive to the politics of the situation.

Certainly your immediate boss and your immediate subordinates should *never* be in category A. To put them there would imply that you were constantly at their beck and call; surely this cannot be right. Most bosses are reasonable people (or like to think they are): if yours rings up and asks you to come immediately to his office, it's perfectly possible to:

(a) ask what it's about – and then challenge the urgency if you think it's justified to do so;
(b) negotiate a later time if you're currently committed

to some other activity which may be jeopardized if it's put to one side. This applies particularly if you're in the middle of a selection or performance review process, a counselling interview, a meeting with your own staff (whose time will be wasted if you disappear indefinitely), or a conversation with customers.

Subordinates (or staff, if you prefer that word) should be trained not to interrupt you every time they feel the inclination to do so, but rather to let a few points pile up until a face-to-face meeting becomes more purposeful and businesslike. If a life-or-death situation arises which does necessitate a sudden interruption from one of your staff, they should be encouraged:

(a) To give a one- or two-sequence statement of what it is they want to see you about, so that you can make an informed judgement about whether it is as Important and Urgent as evidently they believe; and
(b) To make it clear what they want from you. On the whole they will want one of three things, which can be neatly summarized through the acronym 'AID': Advice, Information or Decision. (Sometimes, of course, they don't want anything at all from you, but will claim to be *giving* you information. In reality they are protecting their backs by checking a situation with you to ensure that you implicitly approve of what they plan to do before they actually do it.)

By the way, it follows that if your subordinates should adhere to these principles when approaching you, then you should do the same when tackling your own boss. It also helps if your staff come to you with *solutions* as well as problems, so that they think for themselves.

The people in your 'Avoid' group might include the

staff of the people who work for you. If any of them seek you out, your first question should be 'Have you spoken to your manager/supervisor about this?' If the answer is 'No', then they should be firmly but politely referred to their immediate senior. This holds good even if the supplicant was about to complain about the behaviour of their manager/supervisor, because if they're raising it with you without having given their boss the opportunity to address the situation first, then their boss may feel justifiably aggrieved. All you need to do is ask yourself how you would feel if one of your own people complained about you to your boss without first telling you about the situation and seeking to achieve a mutually acceptable compromise.

Should the response be 'Yes' to your question, then it may still be preferable to deal with the supplicant's manager/supervisor rather than with the supplicant personally. Handling the situation this way may well mean that future problems of the same kind are not sent to you (because the manager/supervisor becomes better equipped to deal with them), but are handled at source, which is the proper place for them.

Insulating Yourself from Interruptions

The range of techniques for preventing interruptions is very wide and to some extent you have to work out your own salvation, based upon your specific work scenario, span of control, and workstation logistics. What is important is to avoid a defeatist attitude about interruptions if you work in an open-plan office, because even here it's possible to reduce the number and flow of gratuitous interruptions, as we shall see. Moreover, everyone has to understand that not all interruptions are unwanted: some are necessary, some are desirable, and some are even welcome. So every point made in the list of ideas below has to be hedged around with caveats and restrictions, as well as with opportunities for creative adaptation and development.

- First of all, ask yourself whether the interrupter is in your category A – the kind of person for whom you drop everything. All your plans for preventing interruptions go by the board for such people.
- You may be able to reorganize your workstation in order to deter potential interrupters and time-wasters. If you currently face an aisle or an array of other workers, you will experience a constant barrage of interruptions or distractions. As people go by, it's the most natural thing in the world for them to stop for a chat. This tendency can be reduced if you reposition your desk so that you have less eye contact with the outside world. Even facing a wall can be preferable to facing other people, though it might be a good idea to fix a small mirror to the blank wall in front of you so that you can see in advance if anyone is approaching you from behind with a threatening expression of their face – or worse still, armed with a knife. The wall (or partition) can also accommodate a sheet of paper on which you have written your value-added mission statement, as a permanent reminder about your priorities.
- If you have staff and/or a secretary, use one of them as your protector against interrupters. Make sure you share with them the names and identities of the people on your A-B-C accessibility list, so that they have some sensible criteria for determining whom to turn away. Conversely, educate people in your 'Restricted' category to approach you via one of your staff or your secretary first.
- Many successful managers initiate a 'surgery hours'

system for coping with interruptions. They make it clear that they are available at certain times (usually at the beginning and the end of the morning and the afternoon), but wish to be left alone at other times unless the issue is one of exceptional urgency and importance – a genuine crisis, in other words.

- In case anyone forgets, the existence of 'surgery hours' can be signalled in various ways. You can display a green card on your desk when you're 'in' for unscheduled visitors, or display a red card when you want to be left alone. If you have an office of your own, the closed or open door can let people know whether you're available or not.

- It makes sense to utilize your personal body rhythms when scheduling times for working on your own. If you find that you do your best thinking or writing in the mornings, then organize your day so that you take advantage of this fact. By contrast, many people are at a low personal ebb immediately after lunch, so it might be a good idea to organize meetings then, in the hope that the stimulus of interaction with others will jolt you out of your inertia. A dose of MBWA (Management By Walking About) can help, too.

- Another point worth remembering is that from the point of view of those who may want to talk to you, the likelihood that they will interrupt you depends on whether they can see you are engaged in activities which they are prepared to regard as *real work*. There are only four activities which count as *real work*:

1. Talking to someone face-to-face;
2. Conducting a conversation on the telephone;
3. Writing; and
4. Working at a keyboard of some description.

- This means if you're fortunate enough to work in an open-plan environment, you can often see potential interrupters striding purposefully towards you and (if they are in your 'Restricted' or 'Avoid' categories) you can initiate one of the *real work* processes (or a possible simulation of them, i.e., a 'pretend' phone call). This is no guarantee against all such interruptions – the potential interrupter may simply hang about in the periphery of your vision, waiting for you to finish whatever you're doing – but it will work some of the time.

- A variant of the 'surgery hours' ploy is to have 'official' and 'unofficial' arrival times at work. Thus you can say that you will be 'officially' in from 9.30 a.m., thereby enabling you to get an hour's work done beforehand.

- Some job-holders are sufficiently senior to be able to work from home for part of the week or whenever they have anything to do which particularly requires original thought. Other job-holders can easily work from home for a good deal of their time, perhaps because they are in the sales function or because they are part of an increasing army of home-based employees with computer links to a head office which may be miles away. For such people, talk of managing face-to-face interruptions is largely irrelevant, but they can still be threatened by the telephone and peremptory incoming messages on the video screen.

- If working from home proves impractical or generates cynical observations from your boss, then it may be possible to work for a while in a quiet and (relatively) secluded part of the organization, like a telephone-free conference room.

- In addition, there are some psychological pointers

worth considering. A reputation for welcoming interruptions will itself generate further interruptions: so it does no real harm to become more directly assertive with time-wasters. Assertiveness also extends to body language like avoidance of eye contact with people whom you sense will start a conversation if you give them the slightest encouragement. Removing the chair (or chairs) positioned conveniently opposite your workstation will deter people who would like nothing better than to sit down and talk to you: either they will go elsewhere (i.e., somewhere they *can* sit down), or their conversation with you will be much briefer than it would have been.

Keeping Interruptions Short

The application of these methods also relies to some extent on your ability to take general principles and turn them into specific techniques relevant to your work situation and environment. Further, there can be no doubt about the fact that the process of managing (i.e., controlling) interruptions means becoming somewhat less 'nice' and somewhat more ruthless. If, hitherto, you've concentrated almost exclusively on being 'nice', then the methods for curbing interruptions will make you feel uncomfortable to begin with: until you find, to your initial amazement, that you can now run your affairs in a more businesslike way without damaging your relationships with colleagues, seniors, subordinates and customers.

- It should be possible to train your own staff to keep to the point and use the time well. The subordinate must:

    (a) Describe the reason for any interruption, i.e. the

66

situation which needs your urgent attention, in one or two sentences.

(b) Indicate what is required from you: Action, Information or Decision.

(c) Suggest some action alternatives or some solutions. Nothing is worse than a subordinate who presents you with problems without making some effort to generate (tentative) solutions. You can always ask: 'What would you do if you were me?'

- Once you know what the interruption is about, you can specify how much time you are prepared to give it, and whether the time will be now or later: 'I think this merits 20 minutes now, or 45 minutes tomorrow afternoon at 3 – which do you prefer?'
- Some managers emphasize the discipline of fixed-time meetings by using an elapsed-time clock or a portable egg-timer. When the clock bleeps or the sand runs out, the interruption is politely but firmly brought to an end.
- Going down the route of fixed-time meetings requires the kind of firm personal discipline which many managers lack. In order to create and sustain credibility, it is vital that meetings scheduled to last for 20 minutes should be ended after 20 minutes, even if the business transaction has not been completed and the meeting has therefore to be reactivated later. Think about it: if you've said that a meeting will last for 20 minutes, and after 45 minutes your interrupter is still with you, what does that do for your credibility the next time you say 'This meeting will last for 20 minutes'?
- Another technique much talked about but seldom tried is to ask people to submit in advance a list of

points to be discussed, on no more than a single side of A4. If you have this list even five minutes before you start the 'meeting' (because, after all, the list is nothing more than an informal 'agenda'), it enables you to prepare your own position more carefully and reduces the need for you to think spontaneously on your feet. The prior organization of ideas on a piece of paper also has other benefits: the case is more systematically presented than would be the case if the visitor simply unleashed a chaotic stream of consciousness, as many do; moreover you can both cut out irrelevant conversation and get on efficiently with the business in hand.

Playing Games With People

Where face-to-face callers are overstaying their welcome (there is a short section on phone calls later in this chapter), then you are at liberty to use the full range of procedural and psychological ploys to bring the interruption to an end. It may seem that some of them come dangerously close to playing games with people, but most of your colleagues, visitors and customers will readily recognize what you are doing and will react without rancour because they are fully capable of using these techniques for themselves.

- The obvious thing to say to an unwanted interrupter is something like 'I can't see you now, please come back in half an hour' or the even more direct 'Go away' (or words to that effect). Being so blatant may be appropriate for callers who fall into your 'Avoid' category, and may even be essential for getting rid of rhinoceros-skinned visitors like double-glazing salesmen or employment agency canvassers. On the other hand, being abrupt with people may be dangerous if

68

they are customers and/or senior to you, and if you wish to maintain good relationships with them. In such cases there is something to be said for being subtle.

- 'Egg-timer eyes' (a glassy stare over the interrupter's shoulder) will help to indicate that your patience is exhausted and that you aren't listening any more. Cleaning your fingernails, doodling or picking the fluff out of your navel are variants.

- Frequent, worried glances at your watch (perhaps coupled with 'My God, is that the time?' or a perplexed tapping of the watch dial as if to check that the hands are still moving) can be a helpful hint to the unsolicited visitor who should be reacting to your body signals. Nervous shuffling of the papers on your desk simply adds to the conspicuousness of the situation.

- Some managers find it useful to preface all their contributions to the conversation with some phrase like 'Well, that seems to wrap it up . . .' or 'That's all for now', perhaps coupled with a decisive closing of the desk diary and switching off the desk light and PC. Again, the visibility of the signal can be enhanced if you stand up and move purposefully towards the door.

- In his book on time management, Derek Torrington argues that if you get up and actually walk out of the room, this will succeed on 100 per cent of occasions in bringing the gratuitous interruption to an end. Unfortunately it will not – indeed, nothing works all the time – because some people will follow you while others will wait for you to return.

- Some visitors are hyper-insensitive. For them, more brutal methods may be permissible. Inviting the caller to engage in a detailed scrutiny of your holiday photographs may sound like a desperate ploy, but with any luck it will remind the interrupter of an urgent appointment elsewhere. If by some mischance they start to settle down with the pictures, you still have an escape route: ask them to bring them back when they've finished.

- On a more serious note, one approach which managers report as being very effective is to make sure when people interrupt you with a problem, they go away with something else additional to the problem they brought to you in the first place. If you develop a reputation for saying something like 'Oh, I'm glad you've dropped in, Mark, because there's something I need you to do for me', then people like Mark will think twice before they make your life a misery. Once they appreciate that you have the capacity and willingness to retaliate, they will suddenly recognize the benefits of solving their own problems.

- Some interruptions are prompted by the caller's desire to discuss last night's television documentary or the football results. In such cases, it is vital that you **do not start a discussion**, but agree with everything that is said to you, however outrageous. In the end, your monosyllabic responses will discourage the visitor and he will go away to find someone more stimulating.

- One last point: if you have to decide between going to a colleague's office (or workstation), or getting him to come to yours, choose the former. True, you are on his territory, but that will make him more comfortable and relaxed, thus encouraging him to lower his guard. What is more important is that you have more control over the duration of the meeting. Even if he doesn't grow more relaxed because he is on home ground, but displays signs of tension because he wants you off his space, you can turn this to his advantage: don't leave until you've got what you came for, or extracted some concession.

Dealing with the Telephone

If there's one almost infallible way of getting through to people in person, it is the use of their direct-line telephone number. [Faxes work almost as well, because of the sense of urgency, significance and immediacy which they generate, but nowadays managers are more switched on to the junk-fax 'problem' and will not automatically drop everything in panic the moment a faxed document hits their desk.] It's almost impossible to resist answering the telephone, and you may think that once you've picked it up, you're doomed to start, continue and terminate a conversation, even if it becomes immediately apparent to you that the caller is someone on your 'Avoid' list or in your 'Restricted' category. However, all is not yet lost. What *can* you do, in practice, to prevent unwanted calls from getting to you, and to 'manage' the ones which do reach you despite your best efforts?

- If you have someone (like a secretary or a nominated 'helpdesk' colleague) who can intercept all your calls and filter them, then clearly it would be foolish not to take advantage of such facilities.
- If you want to be left alone to get on with cerebral work, you may be able to do a deal with one or more colleagues in which they agree to take all your calls (making use of your 'Divert' system) for a pre-determined time. You can always offer to reciprocate at times when a few interruptions would be welcome (e.g., after lunch and at other somnolent moments).
- Telephones which print out the caller's number can

be enormously valuable. Recognizing the number gives you a chance to decide whether to pick up the phone or not, and a further opportunity to prepare yourself if you can guess what the caller is ringing about.

- Some people – mainly among the self-employed – use a similar approach with the aid of answerphones. The answerphone is switched on but with the volume turned up, so that when the caller begins to speak ('after the tone'), you can decide whether to intervene.

- When callers do get through to you, it may be appropriate to devote a little time to the social niceties, but no more time than is absolutely necessary. A lengthy discussion about the weather, forthcoming holidays, the economic situation, hardly seems justifiable if it takes longer than the subsequent work-related talk.

- Monosyllabic responses ('Yes', 'No'), non-committal phrases ('I expect you're right') or wordless grunts all help to discourage excessive conversation. Obviously these tactics can also be used in face-to-face transactions.

- Whatever you do, don't ask open-ended questions, i.e., questions beginning with interrogative words like 'Why'. It's almost impossible for such questions to be answered quickly, even when your respondent is as keen as you are about saving time. If you have to ask questions at all, make them begin with a verb, ('Is that all?') or include a negative ('There's nothing else, is there?').

- The great advantage of the telephone is that your caller cannot see you. It is therefore possible to use a whole range of lies: someone important has just walked in, you're in the middle of a meeting/interview, there's been a bomb warning, the building's on fire. The range of options is only restricted by your imagination, but be careful that you don't tell fibs if your workstation is at one end of a large open-plan office and the person phoning you is at the other end.

Time Management versus 'Customer Service'
Many organizations claim that they give top priority to 'customers' and 'customer service'. Few actually do.

Many give only lip-service to customers: they publish impressive policy statements (like the Citizen's Charter) but they still deter customers from having any contact with managers or other senior people. Further, such organizations seldom allow junior (or low-level) employees the discretion to make the kinds of decisions which would placate dissatisfied customers. Here's a little experiment for you: try phoning any large organization of which you happen to be a customer – a bank, insurance company, local authority, supermarket chain – and ask to speak to the Chief Executive. What will happen is that you will be shunted back and forth by a progression of telephonists, secretaries, marketing people, 'customer service' departments and clerks: *and you will never get to speak to the Chief Executive*, even if you've requested him by name. Now this may be very good time management for the Chief Executive, but it's hardly good service for the customer.

In other words, the pressures for managing time efficiently are often pulling in the opposite direction to the pressures for providing customers with satisfaction. It may seem that the struggle is simply one of those facts of life which we have to cope with, but in reality there are some ways out of the dilemma.

- Low-level employees can be given genuine discretion to make decisions relating to the group of customers for whom they happen to be responsible. Obviously these discretionary powers must themselves have limits, but the exercise of these powers will automatically mean that 80 per cent of customer grievances can be resolved instantly.

- Individual customers must be made aware that they have a named organizational employee who looks after their interests. This person will have his or her name in the signature box at the bottom of correspondence originating from the organization (*not* the name of the departmental manager, who is a figurehead in the sense that he knows nothing about the specific customer and will therefore prove ignorant and unintentionally unhelpful if approached by the customer), with, if necessary, a fabricated job title like 'Customer Service Manager'. Customers with complaints, suggestions or even favourable comments are then more likely to write to, or telephone 'their' contact, at least in the first instance, rather than the Chief Executive.

- Often low-level employees are the people best equipped to answer specific customer queries or complaints anyway, because they are closer to the customer's affairs than anyone else. Recognizing this, and acting on it, will automatically mean that managers can manage their time better because they will have fewer interruptions. What's more, they can devote more time to the interruptions they do have because almost by definition they reflect situations which haven't been resolved earlier in the chain.

Good, positive customer service is *not* inconsistent with effective time management. The two can run in parallel, but only if organizations are prepared to grasp the nettle of empowerment.

CHAPTER 5

How to Train Staff to Leave You Alone

This section explores briefly what bosses typically expect from subordinates, why subordinates frequently fail to deliver, the levels of initiative at which subordinates can justifiably operate, and the importance of making it clear to subordinates how you want them to behave. Obviously, if you don't have staff at the moment, you can skip Chapter Five, but it may come in handy when you eventually become a 'manager' in the more accepted sense of the word.

What has this to do with time management? The answer is simple. If you have people working for you, it will be because you cannot achieve your objectives on your own. The presence of subordinates, therefore, is meant to *reduce* your overall workload, not increase it. If you find that your worries increase as a consequence of having people who are supposed to work for you, then you could be forgiven for wondering about the point of it all. So, first of all, what do we really want from staff?

WHAT DO YOU EXPECT FROM SUBORDINATES?

Managers have *seven* fundamental requirements so far

as their staff are concerned. You could easily imagine that your boss has the same seven requirements of you.

1. **They should willingly obey any orders you may give them.** Many managers shy away from the straightforward issue of orders or instructions, but from time to time it may be necessary (when there is a crisis demanding immediate action, for example). If such scenarios occur – and they should be rare rather than commonplace – then it would be irritating (and time-wasting) almost beyond belief if your staff constantly fought your decisions instead of instantly implementing them to the best of their ability.

    Equally, if a proposal or policy is in its formative/consultative stage, then you should not object at all if your subordinates raise queries, disagree and become Devil's Advocates. If they didn't – if, in other words, your subordinates receive all your judgements, decrees and decisions with uninhibited admiration and uncritical acclaim – then you should start to be very worried: either you are employing zombies, or you are a megalomaniac, or very possibly both. On the other hand, once a proposal or policy has been finalized, then debate should cease and you are entitled to expect that your staff will represent the situation positively and unanimously to the outside world. If they were to do anything else, their actions would be contributing to the possible failure of the policy, and therefore they would be undermining your objectives – which is not what you employ them to do.

    The use of the adverb 'willingly' is quite significant. It suggests that we would prefer it if subordinates applied themselves to their roles with some enthusiasm and commitment, rather than dogged compliance. As managers, we should not expect enthusiasm and commitment to occur automatically: we must work to generate it and then sustain it. In other words we must devote some time to conscious techniques of motivation and leadership, like MBWA.

2. **They should accept you have the right to tell them what to do (and even, if necessary, how to do it).** At one time, the managerial prerogative (the right of management to manage) was well-accepted in hierarchical structures and needed no defence. Today things are different (and getting more different all the time). The acceptance by subordinates of their role can no longer be taken for granted. As a manager you now have to *earn* the right to tell subordinates what to do, and this means making time available to explain your thinking and earn respect.

3. **They should accept your right to criticize them if they do not do as you wish.** This principle sounds unbearably dictatorial because of the way it is worded. What it means in practice is that you expect your staff to perform to certain standards and to achieve agreed objectives; if they do not, then they must expect some feedback and an effort to put them back on the correct path. The fact that your staff do not like to be criticized (nobody does) does not invalidate the process – it simply becomes more difficult. We favour the view of the boss as a learning facilitator (to use a somewhat grandiose phrase): that is, he encourages people to learn from their successes and their mistakes. If staff are given some freedom to make a few decisions, getting them right should justify reward and recognition; getting them wrong should lead to a positive 'learning experience', i.e., some coaching and counselling from the boss. The

question 'Where do you think we went wrong, and what can we do to make sure it doesn't happen again?' is far preferable to the punitive 'Why on earth did you do that?', sometimes accompanied by a stabbing, accusing finger directed at the subordinate's chest. If criticism meant confrontation, in other words, then we would not be in favour of it. The best criticism is self-inflicted, sparked off by personal reflection and the realization of a need to improve; the next best is constructive criticism, unemotional, specific and positive; the worst situation is to receive no feedback at all, even (or especially) when performance is poor.

4. **They should keep you in the picture.** When anything unusual happens, or when the subordinate takes a major initiative, he should tell you about it. Equally, if he has information relevant to your work, he should keep you informed so that you don't make bad decisions (which subsequently have to be reversed or amended) or run into trouble with your seniors. Obviously subordinates must use their judgement when deciding whether to tell you something or not, and sometimes they will get it wrong, but at least the principle is clear. Also the time management implications are obvious. It may cost you some time in the first place if you have to make yourself available to staff who have information for you, but it will save your time in the long run if the quality of your actions is enhanced.

5. **They should not criticize you behind your back.** Ideally, your staff should feel free to criticize you (if they have to) to your face. An important test of healthy senior-subordinate relationships is the extent to which this happens. If you hear that any of your staff are attacking you obliquely, by

denigrating you to others, you are entitled to draw attention to their disloyalty – and to the fact that their behaviour is likely to undermine your effectiveness in the organization. At the same time, loyalty is a two-way transaction: you must be equally loyal to them when speaking about them to the outside world.

6. **They should not purposely get you into trouble.** If your staff derive sadistic pleasure from making mistakes (often not traceable to them) and then watching you pick up the pieces, your time will inevitably be concentrated on Maintenance (fire-fighting). A similar situation occurs when subordinates have developed a mentality in which they simply do what they are told *but no more*. If they see a situation which should demand an immediate response, they will deliberately fail to act, deriving an almost perverse pleasure from your subsequent discomfiture. Clearly you must work hard to undermine such attitudes and behaviour, or prevent them from coming into existence: time spent in this area is a phenomenally profitable investment if it ultimately leaves you free to concentrate almost exclusively on value-added activities.

7. **If you do get into trouble, your staff will do that little bit extra to help out.** It is pleasant to feel that you can rely on your people in an emergency. As with the other principles, you can only expect co-operation if you 'play fair' with your staff.

Indeed, it is a persistent theme with these expectations that if they are to be fulfilled, subordinates must feel there is a reciprocal relationship between you and them – a bit of give-and-take coupled with mutual respect. Any sense of a one-way deal – in which you impose tough standards but give little in return – will soon reap its own reward.

WHY DON'T SUBORDINATES DO WHAT THEY SHOULD DO?

If your people fail to live up to your expectations, there are *four* principal reasons. And, if you accept the conventional principles of managerial accountability, *all of them are your fault*. Thus the first question to ask, when one of your staff does not comply with your criteria, is: *What have I done wrong?* Note that the question is not 'Why are they so stupid?' or 'What makes them so irresponsible?' Because of our powerful ego drives, it is far easier to blame others for our inadequacies than it is to look inwards at ourselves, yet that is precisely what we should be doing. If a subordinate withholds essential information from you, for example, or criticizes you behind your back, it surely makes sense to investigate what *you* have done which has made the subordinate act in these ways. Maybe, more comfortingly, it wasn't you, but it was something your predecessor did, and you are simply viewed as another product from the same mould. Either way, it's up to *you* to alter the situation: leadership by (new) example, coaching, constructive performance feedback, praise and recognition when behavioural change occurs, rewards and incentives when it is consolidated, or the ultimate sanction of departure where the employee is insufficiently responsive.

The four principal reasons for subordinate 'difficulty' are as follows.

1. **They don't know what to do to meet your requirements.** Perhaps you haven't made your expectations,

standards and objectives clear, so your staff are understandably in a state of some confusion.

2. **They don't know how to meet your requirements.** If this is the difficulty, it suggests a need for training, guidance and coaching – with you as the spearhead.

3. **They can't do what is required.** They may have been wrongly selected, in which case the issue is better confronted than left to fester. It may be a more straightforward matter of organization, in which your staff lack the authority to do their jobs effectively – and only you can give them that authority.

4. **They don't want to perform.** In other words, they're not motivated. What you can do on this front depends on the nature of their jobs and their personalities: they may want more stimulating work, they may respond to financial inducements or other tangible incentives, or they may simply feel neglected.

Before you can tackle problems of subordinate inadequacy, you must first assess which of these four causes is responsible. The first two are easier to put right than the others, but all four can be successfully defeated if you concentrate your attention on them.

If we look at the senior-subordinate relationship from another angle, there are five possible levels of initiative which staff can display in that relationship. They are (from the lowest level to the highest):

- The subordinate **waits until told what to do.**
- They **ask what to do.**
- They **recommend** – and await your response.
- They **act and advise you at once.**
- They **act on their own initiative** – and report as a matter of routine.

Any boss worth his salt will outlaw the first two levels. They are completely unacceptable if the manager recognizes that the purpose of having staff is to *increase* the total amount of work done.

The goal must be to produce staff who are capable of acting on their own initiative (within guidelines) and then reporting as a matter of routine. This has to be the most time-effective strategy for both managers and subordinates: it should be kept firmly in mind when recruiting people, training people, appraising people and promoting people. Essentially, what you must do, if you're a manager, is ensure that their monkeys don't become yours.

CHAPTER 6

What's All This Stuff About Monkeys?

When someone – particularly a subordinate or a colleague – approaches you with some opening gambit like 'Have you got a minute?' you can be sure that he has an invisible monkey clinging to his shoulder. You can be equally sure that, given half a chance, he will help that monkey to jump from his shoulder on to yours. It will be your objective to ensure that this does not happen (unless it is one of those rare instances where the monkey is actually yours and has therefore strayed from its legitimate fold).

First of all, when people say 'Have you got a minute?', never has the word 'minute' been more abused. The phrase has a disarming, wheedling quality, designed to persuade you that the forthcoming interruption will take no more than a smidgeon of your time. Once you have consented to the conversation, of course, and have found out that actually it is going to continue for a minimum of five minutes, then it will be too late. So, once again, be on your guard: ask for a one- or two-sentence statement of the 'problem' so that you can judge whether it merits your instant concentration.

Assuming that you've got this hurdle out of the way, the second point to notice is that your visitor will generally embark upon an outline of the situation by claiming that *you* or *we* have a 'problem', The 'problem' is seldom his alone, in other words. Already he is trying to transfer ownership: arguing that the 'problem' is either yours in a personal sense, or yours in the sense that you are accountable for the work of the department as a whole, therefore any work 'problem' encountered in the department is somehow your 'problem' as well.

Of course, this has some truth in it – almost enough to be convincing – but don't forget that you employ people to *solve* 'problems', not simply pass them up to you.

If you wish to keep some control over your value-added time, then you must say something like this to the supplicant:

It is not 'I' or 'we' who have a problem. The problem is yours, and will remain so.

At no time while I am helping you with this or any other problem will your problem become my problem. The instant your problem becomes mine, you will no longer have a problem. *I cannot help someone who doesn't have a problem.*

When this meeting is over, the problem will leave my desk exactly the way it came in – on your back. You may ask my help at any appointed time, and we will jointly decide what the next move will be, and which of us will make it.

In those rare instances where the next move turns out to be mine, you and I will agree it together. I will not make any move alone.

It is often useful to keep a fluffy toy monkey in your drawer, and place it conspicuously on the desk between you and the visitor, drawing attention to the fact that 'this is the literal manifestation of the metaphorical monkey that you have just brought to me'. The toy (which is actually a very valuable executive tool) will remind you forcibly of the dangers of succumbing to any blandishments that you could lead to the monkey being offloaded on to your lap. It may also remind you of the folly of saying things like 'Leave it with me' or 'I'll see what I can do', which signal success for the supplicant because these observations make it clear that the 'problem' has been taken away from him. When the visitor eventually leaves your office or workstation area, make sure that the toy monkey *returns to your desk drawer*, where it can once again sleep the sleep of the untroubled.

Some managers find it tough to adhere to the discipline of the monkey because they take pity on what is obviously a worried person, and they somehow think it unfair that a subordinate should experience stress when they (the manager) are relatively free from it. *Do not succumb to such temptations.* Remember that the supplicant's worried frown, drooping shoulders and despondent voice are largely part of an act deliberately intended to exploit your gullible good nature. If you doubt this, if you consider it cynical, then try a little experiment by giving in to the supplicant just once and say 'Leave it with me' or some similar phrase. You will immediately perceive a smiling countenance (with much more eye contact), erect deportment and upbeat voice as the subordinate is translated from near-suicide to embryonic ecstasy.

Another aspect worth recalling is that if your staff are suffering from worry and stress, you do not help them cope with the situation by taking the worry away from them. It would surely be preferable if they worked the situation through for themselves so that ultimately they develop the kind of (emotional and tactical) self-control that presumably you bring to the work environment. Your job is to help your staff solve their problems, so that they become more effective at future problem-solving: you do not equip your people with problem-solving skills if you constantly take their problems away from them. The only skill they will learn from this process is the ability to bring you more and more 'problems', thereby making them totally dependent on you.

Research on the phenomenon of 'executive stress' suggests that the more senior the manager, the lower is the incidence of stress. Partly, it seems, this is because it is (by and large) only the people who can withstand stress – or even thrive on it – who rise to top positions. Also it is because such people have more staff on whom they can offload their stress – and they are willing to do so.

The concept of the invisible monkey is attractive and endearing. It has led William Oncken and Donald Wass to create 'Five Rules for the Care and Feeding of Monkeys' which are reproduced below because of their importance to all managers concerned about the effective deployment of time. These rules don't just apply to managers, either: at any level you can find you are the unwitting recipient of monkeys dumped by their cunning and devious owners.

1. **Monkeys should be fed or shot.** If you think that a situation deserves to be classified as a 'problem', only treat it as such if you're prepared to do something about it. There's no point in constantly moaning about a 'problem' if you don't confront it and take action to remove it. In other words, if you have to cope with a situation which you don't like, but (you believe) there's nothing you can do about it, your best course of action is to learn to live with it, or learn to work round it.

   Think about the times in the past when you've

joined a meeting whose declared purpose has been to resolve a crisis of some kind. Think about the times when you've sat there, on your own, trying to decide what to do in order to extricate yourself from an unpleasant situation. What proportion of the meeting, or your own thoughts, is wasted by futile speculation about how this 'crisis' could have been avoided if only X had done his job properly? Yet such speculation is completely and utterly futile. Like it or not, the current 'crisis' exists and we cannot remove it simply by wishing that it had not happened. What we must do is distinguish carefully between two questions:

(A) What are we going to do (to resolve the situation)?
(B) What are we going to do to make sure it doesn't happen again?

Question (A) generally requires some urgency, and recriminations about the past serve no purpose. Question (B) can be studied in a more leisurely fashion, and here the search for causes (*not* the search for scapegoats) becomes genuinely relevant.

2. **The monkey population should be kept below the maximum number the manager has time to feed.** If you have four subordinates each unloading three monkeys a day, by the end of the week your office (or workstation) will be crammed with 60 monkeys. You will have to come in on Saturday in order to get rid of them. It will be scant comfort for you to think that at least your staff are having a pleasant, stress-free weekend.

Not only will you have 60 monkeys that you

didn't have before, but they will breed (one is tempted to say like rabbits). Once your people get a taste for passing their monkeys over to you, and once you fall into the habit of accepting them, the practice will grow like some form of dangerous addiction. Far better to equip staff with the ability to solve their own problems: you have more time to yourself, they get more job satisfaction, and 'customers' get better service. Obviously it takes more time at the start if you're going to encourage subordinates to think things through for themselves, instead of supplying them with instant solutions (i.e., the ones which probably worked for you in the past), but the time spent on this activity is a valuable, high-return *investment* by any standards.

3. **Monkeys should be fed by appointment only.** When securing progress and performance feedback from staff, you should do so on a planned and systematic basis. Do not hunt starving monkeys by accosting your people in the corridor and asking them spontaneous questions: you will get little or nothing in return. Often, in fact, you will be given 'good news' noises which may delude you into thinking that things are better than they are.

4. **Monkeys should be fed face-to-face or on the telephone.** The trouble with memos, letters or electronic messages, from your point of view, is that the person sending them has (in effect) disposed of their monkey because it is clinging to the communication. You can pass the monkey back, of course, but it would be preferable if you could have avoided ownership of it in the first place. Should you choose not to reply to the memo/letter/message at all, then the monkey has been shot – but by *you* rather than by its original owner. If it subsequently turns out that the monkey

should not have been shot, you will be blamed for the execution (on the grounds that 'you didn't reply to the memo').

5. **Every monkey should have an assigned 'next feeding time' and 'degree of initiative'.** Agreement on the discretionary freedom and autonomy within which your staff can make their own decisions is a valuable safeguard for your ultimate accountability. Further, the introduction of regular and routine reporting procedures will enable you to keep some grasp of what is going on, and will avoid a constant sequence of one-off interventions by subordinates anxious to keep you 'up to date'.

[Note: The 'Five Rules for the Care and Feeding of Monkeys' are copyright 1974 by the President and Fellows of Harvard College; all rights reserved. Reprinted with permission of the *Harvard Business Review*. 'Management Time: Who's Got the Monkey?' by William Oncken, Jr, and Donald L. Wass, appeared in the *Harvard Business Review*, November–December 1974.]

CHAPTER 7

Breaking the Delegation Barrier

INTRODUCTION

If you have staff working for you, delegation is one of the best ways of saving your time and allowing you to put some of it to more productive, 'value-added' uses. Virtually all managers support the idea of delegation *in principle* – the surprising thing is that so few managers practise what they preach. Fortunately, organizational fashion in the 1990s – decentralization and devolution, flattened hierarchies with larger spans of control, the doctrine of empowerment – is forcing managers to delegate more if they are retain their sanity, but even so there is often room for further and spectacular improvement.

Even if you don't have people working for you, you may be able to make use of some of the techniques for effective delegation, so please don't pass by this chapter on the grounds that it doesn't apply to you.

WHAT IS DELEGATION?

Delegation is entrusting responsibility and authority to others (normally your subordinates) who then become *responsible* to you for their results. You remain *account-able* to your boss for what your subordinates do (and for what *their* subordinates do, incidentally, and so on ad infinitum).

What you delegate, essentially, is **the right to make decisions.** So delegation is *not* merely the passing downwards of work. Here are two ways of dealing with a customer complaint:

Strategy A: You ask one of your staff to 'get the facts'.

When the facts are reported, you decide what action to take and instruct the subordinate to respond to the complaint in accordance with your solution.

Strategy B: You ask one of your staff to investigate and then deal with the issue as they consider appropriate, so long as (1) the customer's grievance is resolved and (2) the customer is tied more closely to your organization than was the case before. The subordinate then reports on the action taken as part of a routine feedback system.

Strategy A involves no delegation; *Strategy B* incorporates lots of it. These are not the only alternatives, of course: you could ask a subordinate to investigate and then generate recommendations, which would be a halfway house between full delegation and no delegation at all. The important point is that in either case, if the subordinate fails to deliver acceptable results, you can grab the delegated responsibility back again, or redefine the objective, or introduce more effective control procedures. Delegating to someone other than a subordinate can create difficulties of control over the results, and that is why it is a practice which we do not recommend, as you can find yourself accountable for something which you can no longer manage.

If delegation isn't merely passing work downwards,

then equally it isn't merely the downward transmission of *authority*. Some managers argue that you can't pass *responsibility* to staff, because whatever happens you remain responsible to your boss for what they do: how can you give something away and simultaneously keep it? Yet to think along these lines is to fail in recognizing the crucial difference between *responsibility* and *accountability*. You are *responsible* upwards for what you personally do and achieve; you are *accountable* upwards for what your staff do and achieve.

If you were to dispense *authority* without *responsibility*, think about the implications. What you would be saying, in effect, is 'I'm giving you the freedom to take certain decisions, but I'm not going to hold you responsible for the outcome.' What subordinates would not jump at such an opportunity: to take decisions without any risk of being held to account? Equally, what sort of boss would knowingly give people carte blanche to take initiatives, and then take the consequences of what these people actually do? Yet there are still plenty of examples, in organizations, where managers do have the freedom to exercise authority without responsibility: in some cases, even now, personnel officers select staff and allocate them to other parts of the organization without ever being responsible for the results of their decisions.

Responsibility without *authority* is an equally bizarre combination: 'I'm going to hold you responsible for the outcome of doing X, but I'm not giving you any freedom or discretion in the situation.' Small wonder that responsibility without authority has been described as a do-it-yourself hangman's kit.

To summarize: delegation is the passing downwards of decision-making authority and responsibility. You remain unavoidably accountable for the decisions made and their outcomes, a fact which straight away suggests the necessity for *control*. So delegation is not a sink-or-swim process: it must be carefully planned, implemented and supervised. Let nobody imagine that *delegation* and *abdication* are synonyms.

WHY DELEGATE?

There are both *good* (morally virtuous) and *bad* (selfish) reasons for delegating. You might delegate a particular responsibility, for example, because you don't like doing it or don't know how to do it (and can't be bothered to learn), though neither of these reasons needs to be communicated to the subordinate who takes on the work involved. You might delegate, too, in order to place a particular person under pressure, not as a means of testing his mettle but rather as a technique for encouraging his early departure. We shall confine ourselves here, however, to a discussion of the *good* reasons.

1. **Delegation equips staff to solve their own problems.** In this way everyone (including you) is used to their maximum potential, and the overall effectiveness of you and your team is maximized. When subordinates seek to unload their problems in your direction, remember all the advice about monkeys in the previous chapter.
2. **Delegation gives you more time for adding value.** Remember the four roles of the employee: Maintenance, Crisis Prevention, Performance Improvement and Change Management. If you don't delegate enough, you're liable to devote far too much time to activities which don't add value; Performance Improvement and Change Management are neglected.

3. **Delegation makes you dispensable.** In principle, it is only dispensable people who get promoted. From the organization's standpoint, it wants everyone to be dispensable because this means that corporate effectiveness is unimpaired when staff drop dead or leave unexpectedly. We appreciate that in some companies the dispensable individual is an easy target for redundancy, but this is the exception rather than the rule. The indispensable manager may keep his job, but he won't get promoted, and he is a constant threat to the organization's continuity or even its survival.

4. **Delegation helps you motivate your staff and assess their potential.** The planned transfer of authority and responsibility can help you to retain the interest of your subordinates – and ultimately to retain the subordinates themselves. Some will believe that delegation amounts to exploiting the individual because you are asking him to assume extra responsibilities without any commensurate increase in the financial rewards associated with the job. There are two responses to this objection. First, if the subordinate performs well, he will eventually be upgraded or promoted, thereby restoring equilibrium between his role and his salary. Second, very few subordinates ever complain about too many responsibilities being given to them; they are much more prone to complain about the absence of delegation.

WHY IS IT SO HARD TO DELEGATE?

Clearly there are genuine reasons why managers can't delegate. If you have no staff, then (according to our definition) delegation becomes a physical impossibility –

though it may still make sense for you to dispose of some activities elsewhere, if you can. There may be certain responsibilities which you must perform yourself – because the law says you must, or company policy dictates it – and clearly you must comply. If there are some responsibilities which you think should be delegated but which your boss insists must be done personally by you, you are entitled to try to persuade him to change his views, but if you fail you have an obligation to do as he wishes.

Although these caveats have more or less universal application, they can be broken from time to time. For example, we have known instances where managers have hidden behind 'company policy' as a reason for not delegating performance appraisal to intermediate levels of supervision between them and clerical staff (in a large financial services organization). Other managers, by contrast, have recognized that 'company policy' is indefensible on this issue and have courageously delegated the performance appraisal process to their supervisors on the understandable grounds that nobody is better equipped to assess the achievements of the clerks under their control. In this company, therefore, 'company policy' became increasingly out of step with managerial practice, to the point where eventually 'company policy' was changed to reflect what had by then become the status quo.

So even the so-called genuine reasons for failing to delegate are less authentic than they might at first appear. In the majority of instances, moreover, managers fail to delegate for reasons founded on fear or ignorance, or fear and ignorance combined. This situation in fact represents an opportunity, because it implies some potential for change if only the fear can be removed and the ignorance replaced by self-confidence.

Let's look more closely at the most typical barriers to effective delegation.

1. **The delegator doesn't clearly understand where his own authority and responsibility begin and end.** If you're uncertain about the precise content of your job, then you can't delegate properly.
2. **The delegator thinks he can do the work better than his staff.** It may even be true that you can do the job better than your staff. Yet that in itself is no argument for performing these tasks yourself, particularly if it means that you devote less time to the parts of the job which are exclusively yours, i.e., the parts which add value. Remember, too, that where someone is inadequate, their performance will never improve if you do their work for them. Instead, they must be shown where they have gone wrong and required to do the job again; if that is impractical, they must be given the same kind of task at the earliest opportunity in the future. At all times you must watch for the people who deliberately pretend to be incompetent in the hope that some distasteful parts of their role will be taken away from them; regrettably this ploy often succeeds. What should happen is the clear and decisive transmission of the message that the quickest way to get rid of a task is to do it properly, because making a mess of it (deliberately or otherwise) will simply mean that you'll have to do it again.
3. **The delegator feels insecure.** These feelings manifest themselves in a variety of ways. You may be afraid of not being essential; you may prefer to perform routine duties in your 'comfort zone' rather than the more demanding and challenging tasks of the value-added manager; you may be frightened of appearing

lazy to your staff, to your peers, to your boss, or even to yourself (in the latter case, fear takes the form of guilt). It takes a secure and self-confident person to run the risks associated with delegation; but if you don't delegate, the risks are even greater, to yourself, your staff, your boss and your career.

Many managers fail to delegate because they realize that if delegation is the right to make decisions, then it incorporates the freedom to make mistakes – and they are frightened of the consequences of these mistakes. To delegate properly, you must be confident that you can solve any problem that your subordinates may generate. That in turn highlights the importance of timely and effective control measures once the process of delegation has been initiated.

4. **The delegator believes in the exercise of authority and the managerial prerogative.** Increases in unemployment have encouraged a resurgence of the managerial prerogative – the belief that managers have a right to manage and that the role of subordinates is to do what they are told. Managers operating in this fashion become indispensable (and are therefore incompetent), while subordinates become sullen, alienated and disillusioned, fighting the 'system' by subversively undermining the manager's decisions. Dialogue between manager and subordinate is discouraged and overall productivity is poor.

5. **The delegator believes that subordinates are already overworked.** So how can they possibly do more? There are several positive answers to this question.

- It may be that the delegator's claim about overworked subordinates is itself nothing more than a pretext, a defence mechanism disguising the delegator's reluctance to delegate.

- If staff are genuinely overworked (or appear to be), the manager must look closely at what they are doing to determine whether some of it can be jettisoned altogether, some can in turn be delegated further down the organization, or some tasks can be performed more efficiently and therefore occupy less time.
- It's noticeable that even when subordinates claim to be overworked, they can always find time to do something *that they want to do.* Statements about being overworked are often little more than a smokescreen. There is some truth in the old proverb that if you want something done quickly, give it to a busy person!

THE SYSTEMATIC APPROACH TO DELEGATION

1. **Agree the scope of your job with your boss.** Unless you have a clear idea about the limits of your authority and responsibility, you cannot delegate.
2. **Clarify with your staff exactly what you expect from them.** They should all be aware of the limits of their authority and responsibility, and they should certainly know the standards of performance which will be considered acceptable.
3. **Specify the delegated objective.** The objective should be what it says it is, i.e., the *result* you want. It should incorporate the absolute minimum of direction on the *methods* to be used in accomplishing the objective. If people don't have any freedom to determine the best way of producing the result, then the process ceases to be delegation and becomes the mere allocation of a task.

When putting together an objective, it is important to avoid weasel words and phrases like 'as soon as possible' (which can mean anything from 'yesterday' to 'never') because they give little guidance to staff needing direction on priorities.

The ingredients of a meaningful objective should satisfy the **TRAMPS** criteria:

T Time-bounded
Is there a target date for completion (or 'milestones' to enable progress to be measured)?

R Result-oriented
Is the delegated responsibility compatible with the individual's Key Tasks or Key Result Areas? Will it add value?

A Attainable
Are the deadline and specified standards achievable?

M Measurable
Do we have quantifiable ways of establishing whether the objective has been satisfactorily achieved (other than the deadline)?

P Precise
Does the objective relate to some specific area of activity? Is the outcome clearly defined?

S Stretching
Does the objective constitute a challenge for the subordinate?

Make sure you apply the **TRAMPS** model to your own objectives when delegating systematically.

4. **Give your staff the means of carrying out what is required of them.** If your people are to perform delegated responsibilities effectively, they must have the resources and equipment to enable them to do so.

These may include training, tools, machines, materials, people (to make up a project team, for example) and perhaps the right to spend some money.

5. **Set up effective and timely control systems.** The frequency of progress reports is a matter for common sense, but depends on the following factors:

- The time-scale for completion of the delegated task.
- Your confidence in the subordinate.
- Your purpose in delegating: you may be deliberately trying to find out how the subordinate will fare when left largely on his own.
- The significance of the delegated task in organizational terms.

What is more important is that progress reports should consist of more than a brief exchange of words in the corridor. You must insist on seeing tangible evidence of what has been done so far, and secure specific feedback on what is planned for the next stage. This is why delegated projects should have prescribed 'feeding times'.

It is equally important to avoid the trap of over-delegating to people who have a competent track record, and failing to delegate to others who have proved themselves to be unreliable, or who have no track record at all. The competent people may end up as unwilling 'specialists' in, say, report-writing, merely because they produced one or two persuasive reports in the recent past – and the unreliable people remain unreliable (or untried) because they are never given the chance to redeem themselves.

6. **Reward the people who get things done.** You cannot delegate unless your staff are prepared to accept

additional responsibility. They will accept responsibility and actively participate in accomplishing the objectives of the organization only if they feel that rewards go to the people who get things done. The extent of such rewards is not restricted solely to those which are officially sanctioned by the organization (like annual increments), but also encompasses a range of initiatives which can be taken by the individual manager. Some words of genuine and sincere appreciation, for example, can be highly effective; other options include some unofficial time off, the chance to be departmental delegate to a conference, a change of job title, or some visible exposure by acting as your representative in some regular management committee and project team.

It is crucial to recognize that *the rewards for being right must always be greater than the penalties for being wrong*. If a subordinate makes a mistake, it may be hugely enjoyable (and even therapeutic – for you) if you walk round him for half an hour, commenting imaginatively on his ancestry. What he will learn from this experience is that taking risks (the risks inherent in any decision-making) is dangerous and can lead to unpleasant consequences. The best way to avoid any repetition of these unpleasant consequences is not to take decisions in the future – in other words, not to accept delegated responsibilities. If your staff take this attitude, then *you have failed as a manager*.

You must resist the desire to over-criticize when subordinates make mistakes, especially if they have been brought up to rely on authority. Instead, it will be more profitable to engage in a non-emotional analysis using questions like 'Where did we go wrong?' and 'What can we both do to make sure it doesn't happen again?' The use of the pronoun 'we' in these questions is not some none-too-subtle form of psychological manipulation, but stems from the manager's realization that if the subordinate has failed to produce acceptable results, the causes are as likely to be the manager's own inadequate briefing, coaching, training and control.

7. **Use delegation as a means of developing your staff – and freeing yourself for more important (value-added) things.** Regular performance appraisal (whether your organization has a formal system or not) supplies an opportunity for producing a 'balance sheet' to record achievements, progress and needs for further improvement. Sitting down with individual subordinates every six months or so to discuss overall performance may well suggest pointers for future delegation in new and previously unexplored dimensions of the person's role. What's more, you may learn something about yourself: maybe your objective-setting tactics are too dictatorial, or you could have been more helpful at times when the subordinate was struggling.

WHAT SHOULD YOU DELEGATE?

Clearly we cannot answer this question comprehensively in the context of a general set of guidelines. However, the overall principles suggest that you should delegate anything which your staff can do:

1. **Better than you** – because they are younger, fitter, more recently qualified, or have strengths in areas where you are weak. Ask yourself these questions:

- Are you taking full advantage of key people with more knowledge and experience than you in certain aspects of the work?
- Have you looked in the mirror lately, assessed your own strengths and weaknesses, and then utilized the resources available to you in order to compensate for your own inadequacies?
- So far as your unit's 'customers' are concerned, will they actually get a better service if they deal with your staff rather than with you, because your staff know each 'customer' in greater depth?

2. **At less expense than you** – because they are paid less than you. If they tackle something that previously you did yourself, then the overall 'cost' to the organization has been reduced – and there is always the possibility of enhanced 'profit' if you allocate the time saved to more value-added projects.

3. **With better timing** – because they are on the spot. Again, so far as 'customers' are concerned, it's likely that your staff can give immediate service whereas your response will be delayed because of your need to ask questions and sift information before you can respond to queries and complaints.

4. **As part of their normal functions** – because whatever we're talking about, it's *their* job rather than yours, and even if they don't do it well to begin with, they won't improve if you take it away from them. So, for example, your subordinates should manage and control their staff, not you. Remember, too, that each job should be handled at its lowest possible level – and that level is probably lower than many managers think it is.

5. **As a contribution to their training and development** – because people constantly need to be stretched if

their interest in the job is to be sustained. Further, the world itself is changing, with increased competitiveness pressures, more challenges, new techniques, higher expectations about performance. Your staff have to be prepared for this future: delegation will help them to cope.

6. **To assess their suitability for promotion** – because it's often a huge mistake to promote people simply because they're good at what they're doing now, if the next job up is significantly different. Think about high-performing sales representatives who become poor-performing sales managers. If you want to find out whether someone will be a successful manager (or project leader, or whatever) then give them a taste of the role and watch how they react.

WHAT SHOULD YOU NOT DELEGATE?

The things you mustn't delegate are the things that only you can do. They include:

1. **Overall policy and planning for your area of responsibility.** If words like 'policy' and 'planning' seem very grand to you, or even irrelevant on the grounds that people much higher up your organizational ladder are responsible for these things, then please remember that 'policy' and 'planning' *do* apply to you:

- 'Policy' means making it clear to your staff what you expect from them: not only in terms of results, but also, where appropriate, in terms of behaviour, appearance, discipline, readiness to take initiative, and so on.

- 'Planning' implies the allocation and control of delegated duties, the organization of your own time, and the establishment of routines for yourself and your team.

2. **A concentrated focus on your value-added priorities.** This means that your own time is best deployed if you focus constantly on ways of doing your job *better, faster* and *cheaper* (i.e., Performance Improvement), and on doing new things (i.e., Change Management). If you're in charge of an internal service function, for example, it is you who must constantly seek 'customer' feedback, evaluate it, and prod your unit into enhancing standards; it is your role, too, to market and sell your function within the organization, perhaps with the aid of some market research and pilot-testing for new services.

3. **Selection, training and performance appraisal for your immediate subordinates.** In principle, it would be an abrogation of your managerial accountability to allow any of these functions to be carried out for you by someone else.

4. **Promotion, praise and discipline for your immediate subordinates.** Obviously promotions and upgradings may be subject to organizational policies and the decisions of others, but this does not stop you from making recommendations and from trying to influence outcomes.

5. **Anything your immediate boss wants you to do personally.** As we've already seen, you may resist if you think that your boss is misguided, but if your arguments are rejected then you have little option but to comply.

6. **Leadership for your people.** Whether you like it or

not, your staff will look to you for some leadership: they may even see you as their role model. Certainly they will do so if they perceive some discrepancy between what you do personally and what you're requiring from them. So you cannot delegate your leadership function to someone else. Even to contemplate the possibility and the consequences shows how absurd it would be.

7. **Final accountability for the work of your team.** You can't delegate this under any circumstances.

In addition, of course, you should not delegate anything to people who are genuinely not capable of doing the work, or to people who do not work for you.

CONCLUSION: LET'S GET THE MESSAGE CLEAR

Delegation isn't the same as abdication. It does *not* mean giving someone a task, with the minimum of guidance and control, and then leaving them to sink or swim. This approach leaves too much to chance, is wasteful of time and effort, and (what's worse) exposes the manager too much.

Delegation *is* a question of distinguishing between the urgent and the important. So much of a manager's time may be consumed in performing the *urgent* tasks which clamour for attention that there is little time left to do the *important* (value-added) things. The strongest argument for delegation, in fact, is that it leaves the delegator free to concentrate on more significant issues. Only if you free yourself from operational details will you have the time necessary for the genuinely managerial functions of planning, organizing, leading and controlling.

Delegation *is* a matter of not behaving like any of the well-known Birds of Delegation, whose habitats are often located in the middle and upper reaches of the managerial ladder.

The White-Shirted Hoverer
The bird who gives people jobs to do and then perches on their shoulders.

The Pin-Striped Whoopster
The bird who, like the Hoverer, watches closely over subordinates and becomes very raucous when they deviate from the way *he* thinks the job should be done.

The Yellow-Bellied Credit Snatcher
A bird who is often highly regarded.

The Lesser White-Crested Cuckoo
The bird who's only too anxious to lay eggs in the other person's nest.

The Duck-Billed Double-Talker
The bird who never makes it entirely clear how much authority he intends to delegate.

The Golden-Crowned Mourning Dope
The bird who constantly complains about the inability of subordinates to make decisions, and never lets them decide anything.

The Black-and-White Organization Creeper
The bird who delegates authority and then creeps round the structure to lower-level staff, thereby nullifying the delegation.

The Red-Headed Fire-Fighter
The bird who thinks he does delegate, but makes his people check with him before making even the most minor decisions.

The Lion-Kicking Vulture
The boss who sits back and waits for subordinates to make mistakes, and then kicks them.

CHAPTER 8

Time Management and the Art of Managing the Boss

Not only must you successfully manage your time with your staff, with your peers and your 'customers', but you must also manage your time with your boss. If anything, managing the boss is more crucial to your career than anything else, and therefore it deserves special attention in this manual.

In this section, therefore, we shall first assess what bosses typically expect from their subordinates, and what you can do to ensure that you make a good job of managing the time you have with your boss. Along the road we will also look at some of the reasons why some senior-subordinate relationships don't prove successful. As you read what follows, you might usefully think about the extent to which *you* fulfil the requirements of an effective boss, and whether *you* are guilty of any of the 'sins' which bosses sometimes commit, and your own capacity to improve so far as your staff are concerned.

WHAT PEOPLE EXPECT FROM THEIR BOSSES

The following six components of the effective senior-subordinate relationship are phrased as direct quotations because they are often, more or less, what people say when asked how they would like their boss to behave towards them. There is nothing particularly novel, original or startling about the list: what is startling is the depressingly large number of occasions on which seniors don't supply the ingredients needed to enable their people to operate effectively.

1. **'I want to know what the boss expects from me.'** If you are to apportion your own priorities sensibly, you have to know the objectives you are expected to achieve, the specific tasks (if any) you have to undertake, the priorities attached to these objectives and tasks by your boss, and the criteria which will be used in judging your performance.

2. **'I want the opportunity to discuss my activities, targets and performance standards.'** Preferably your workload will not simply be a matter of hierarchical imposition, although now and again this is unavoidable if, for example, the organization is up against it and drastic steps must be taken, quickly, in order to survive. Just as your boss has some objectives he wants you to take on board, you may have some ideas of your own for which you would like to gain his commitment.

3. **'I want to be allowed to be effective.'** You need the resources essential to the accomplishment of your objectives: guidance, support, coaching. It is important, too, that your boss does not interfere with your own managerial responsibilities by communicating directly with your subordinates (other than purely in a social capacity).

4. **'I want him to show some interest in what I am doing.'** Now and again it would be encouraging to think that the boss values your services and will

discuss your progress with you. Armed with such feedback, you can manage your time more effectively and confidently because you know (a) what you're doing well, (b) where you need to improve, and (c) what you need to do differently.

5. **'I want prompt information about changes affecting me and my staff.'** Nothing is more annoying (and time-wasting) than to learn about new directions and policy changes *after* you and your team have embarked on the implementation of previously-agreed plans.

6. **'I want to be treated like a human being.'** Because the senior-subordinate relationship is founded on reciprocal obligations, you expect the boss to make some allowance for the fact that you are a human being (just as you make similar allowances for him), and that you have a life outside work which occasionally takes precedence.

WHERE DO BOSSES GO WRONG?

Before you can tackle the difficulty of the less-than-perfect boss, you have to isolate precisely what is wrong. Here are six typical manifestations of managerial inadequacy which bosses can display – unfortunately the list is not comprehensive.

1. **The boss is never available.** Either the boss is 'out' altogether, committed to mysterious errands, or his presence is required continually at meetings, or he is simply unpunctual, inefficient and unreliable because of poor personal organization. Major problems remain unresolved and decisions cannot be taken until the prodigal son returns; value-added initiatives

go into cold storage; there is inadequate integration within the team; infrequent communication leads to whimsical policy changes and a substantial waste of time and effort. When such bosses *are* available, it is usually first thing in the morning and last thing at night, so staff take to lurking in the car park, or waiting around hopefully in the evenings, in order to catch a moment with their leader.

2. **The boss never tells you anything.** Often this is linked to lack of availability, but the connection is not inevitable: with some bosses, even their physical presence is no guarantee that necessary information will be forthcoming. You may find, therefore, that you hear about policy or system changes from your own staff, or you learn about them by chance meetings in the corridor, or you discover them when you are being chastised by a boss who thinks you should have known about them anyway.

3. **The boss keeps changing his mind.** Managers don't appreciate that subordinates tend to hang on to every word. A chance remark, therefore, can set in motion a burst of irrelevant staff activity; subordinates become confused and uncertain, not knowing in which direction to move and consequently hedging their bets by moving a little bit in all directions simultaneously. Once more, time is wasted in abortive projects.

4. **The boss tries to do your job as well as his own.** Interference with subordinate work can either be intermittent or persistent: either way it generates delays and needless repetition. It often results from a recent promotion, where the boss lacks the wider perspective required for his new role and retreats back into the 'comfort zone' of the post he has just (in theory) vacated. So far as you are concerned,

your autonomy is sabotaged, especially if the interference is persistent, while your personal development is slowed down. The fact that the development of your boss is also slowed down is small consolation.

5. **The boss takes all the credit.** Of course, if we adhere to the principle of accountability, your boss is entitled to claim credit for your achievements – but not to act as if you made no contribution whatsoever. The consequence of the plagiarizing, parasitical manner is that you remain unknown to some of the people who ought to matter in your life if your career is to be successful.

6. **The boss declines to tell you how you are doing.** This may arise because the job is ill-defined at the outset or because the boss simply does not give you adequate guidance and feedback. Persistent ambiguity of this kind produces stress, especially in cases where your view of your effectiveness, and your manager's view, are poles apart. The result can be irreparable harm to your career prospects, and even redundancy or dismissal.

WHAT CAN YOU DO TO CHANGE YOUR BOSS?

We once saw this notice on an office wall:

Rules for Managing the Boss
Rule 1 The boss is always right
Rule 2 When the boss is wrong, refer to Rule 1.

There is a grain of cynical truth here, but it is worth remembering that most unhappy subordinates are the victims of haste, insensitivity or plain thoughtlessness, rather than vindictiveness or calculated unfairness. Our approach relies on the accuracy of this assumption. If you are genuinely the target of malice from your boss, then your remedies (in so far as any exist) are somewhat different from those listed below.

Also, you must not admit defeat. You must believe that it is actually possible to define the changes you would like to see in the ways your boss manages you, and then to initiate plans that will bring about these changes. If you believe the situation is hopeless and that you are helpless, then of course nothing will change.

1. **Before you do anything, remember your main objective.** Your purpose is to create a *working relationship which permits optimum job performance*. Stealth is preferable to haste, especially as action which is too purposeful may be seen as threatening, and almost any form of confrontation will prove counter-productive. So you should work hard to keep your emotions under control, especially if one of these emotions is anger: think carefully about the words you intend to use when discussing issues with your boss, try to anticipate his reactions and have your responses ready, and learn to express yourself in a calm voice with 'open' body language. It may be helpful to enlist the assistance and co-operation of colleagues whose view of the boss is the same as yours, because collectively you can together wield far more influence than any one of you can do on your own. (Incidentally, if you find that your view of the boss is *not* shared by your colleagues, then the cause of your problem is far more likely to lie with you

than with the boss, and you must therefore look at your own behaviour, personality and performance first.)

2. **Establish a clear aim.** It may be that you have to persuade your boss to spend more time at his desk so that he can concentrate on clarifying currently ambiguous policies. Alternatively you may want to start an arrangement which allows you half an hour a week with your boss in order to review progress and agree future actions. Whatever you want to change, it's not enough to know what is wrong: you have to know what is right as well – you have to know your *objective*.

3. **Seek a written definition of your role.** Job definitions help to specify and protect autonomy; if produced properly, they indicate the (value-added) reason for your existence, and they list your Key Result Areas, or those responsibilities which account for the major part of your success. Job definitions also help to circumscribe the activities of the boss because they should suggest (if only by implication) what is yours and what is his.

    If your boss is unwilling to produce a written definition of your role, write one for yourself and invite his reactions. You'll get them! A word of advice, however: write a specification for your role which gives you maximum discretion and autonomy. If you gain acceptance for this version, you will then enjoy considerable freedom and scope, not only for yourself but also for the people who work in your team. Don't produce a detailed, all-embracing job description listing every possible aspect of your duties. Many organizations don't like them because they are restrictive, they sound negative, and they encourage resistance to change.

4. **Manage the information flow.** Use information to reassure your boss, to confirm that you are doing your job as he would have it done. Bosses need information if they are to make sensible decisions themselves, so it does not help your relationship with your boss if you give him any sudden surprises. Even pleasant surprises are unwelcome because the next surprise may not be pleasant. Of course, if you hide a problem from your boss and the problem goes away, you will have protected yourself from a potential admission of inadequacy. On the other hand, if the hidden problem doesn't go away, and eventually the boss learns about it from another source, he will now have two sticks to beat you about the head with: the problem itself, and your failure to keep him informed.

5. **Insist on consistency.** The language here sounds strong, but this rule applies especially in those scenarios where the boss appears to say something one day and then contradict himself the next. You have to safeguard your interests here. You can do it, for example, by conspicuously taking notes at meetings with your boss and then reading back your proposed actions, or by sending confirmation memos to your boss just to make sure that you've fully understood what he wants you to do. At worst, you may have to add something like 'Unless I hear from you within two days, I will assume that my version of our agreed Action Plan is correct, and I will proceed accordingly.'

6. **Promote confidence in yourself.** If your boss does interfere in what you're doing, you have to ask yourself why he does so. Perhaps it's not so much that he used to do your job, but rather that he lacks confidence in you. Why does he lack confidence? Maybe the causes lie in your track record of missed dead-

lines, forgotten tasks, lateness at meetings, lack of preparation for important discussions, inability to present your arguments convincingly, and lost papers. The remedies are self-evident: move heaven and earth to meet deadlines, keep diary notes so that tasks are not forgotten, turn up on time for meetings (preferably a little bit beforehand), allocate time for thorough preparation, learn (and practise) presentation techniques, and create an efficient filing system. If you become credible in the eyes of your boss, it's virtually certain he will leave you alone much more.

7. **Help build a team.** One of your senior's tasks is to integrate the activities of you and your colleagues, so that you all have a common purpose. If you can contribute positively to the team-building process, you then help your boss, your colleagues and above all yourself. Thus a fortnightly team meeting may be a good idea, particularly if it enables the subordinates as a group subtly to put collective pressure on the boss to modify his style and behaviour.

8. **The boss must be treated as a human being.** If he has foibles and personal idiosyncrasies, then it may be sensible to pander to them, especially if it helps you to get what you want from him. If he is a *reader*, make sure your ideas are sent to him in written form before you go in to discuss them; if he is a *listener*, there should be no problem about raising issues spontaneously. Learn about 'word magic': with most people there are certain words which give off a positive resonance (like 'total quality' and 'empowerment'), while others will cause the shutters to come down. Peter Drucker says that he once worked for an engineer who hated the word 'control' but loved the word 'measurement': you soon discovered which one to use.

9. **Manage your time with the boss: ensure that it's productive.** You must not monopolize the time of your boss, but you are entitled to his advice, and you will get it provided you've done your homework first by adhering to these simple guidelines:

- When you are about to approach your boss, clarify your objective firmly in your mind: do you want Advice, Information or a Decision?
- Never present problems without indicating some possible solutions and even your own preferred course of action. You may find that your own ideas go down well, with the result that you're left to get on with it.
- Time your interventions in order to minimize inconvenience to your boss. If he operates a 'surgery hours' pattern of operation, then comply with it unless the matter is life-or-death.
- Take note of whether the boss prefers infrequent but longer meetings, or ad hoc sessions.
- Get to the point quickly.
- Anticipate objections and questions: have your responses ready.

CHAPTER 9

Saving Time at Meetings

The purpose of this section is simply to draw attention to the time management aspects of meetings and discussions. It does not set out to equip you with chairmanship or discussion-leading skills, except in the sense that such techniques are relevant to the control of time spent working face-to-face with others.

Certainly no organization can survive without formal and informal meetings, conferences, committees and discussions. The larger the organization, the greater is the need to make use of meetings. John Mole's book, *Mind Your Manners* (Industrial Society, 1990), has a series of chapters about the culture, management style and corporate characteristics of business behaviour in European countries. In the section on the United Kingdom, the author states:

'*Meetings are the most important and time-consuming management tool. Only the least important decisions or instructions are not formulated, discussed, approved, ratified, communicated, implemented at a meeting. They are not regarded as interruptions from real work. It is not acceptable to leave a meeting halfway through, make phone calls, get on with paperwork.*'

Meetings are the target of some feeble witticisms among UK managers, who may believe that 'The camel is a horse designed by a committee' and that 'The best meeting is a meeting of two people, with one of them absent.' The regular utterance of such one-liners does not inhibit managers from continuing to convene or attend meetings, however. Indeed it is profoundly ironic that while many managers complain about the meetings they attend or run, describing them as largely a waste of time, in principle a meeting, properly organized and run, can be a vital tool for *saving time* and achieving results.

First of all, what is a meeting? We define a meeting straightforwardly as a gathering of two or more people designed to achieve an objective. So most forms of interview (for selection, appraisal and so forth) can legitimately be construed as meetings, according to the definition; indeed we argue that it would be beneficial to see such events as meetings because we could then design them as such, with properly-prepared agendas and subsequent action notes. Clearly meetings vary enormously: in the numbers attending, the formality of the procedure, the explicit presence of a chairperson, adherence to legalistic rules, seating patterns, production of (and adherence to) agendas and responsibility for follow-up. Some meetings are better described as 'discussions', still others as 'committees', but such semantic niceties need not bother us here.

We know that some people abhor meetings, in spite (or perhaps because) of attending a great many of them. We can take these objections about meetings with a pinch of salt, however, because if expressed dissatisfaction about meetings was as strong as is sometimes claimed, managers would have found better ways to make decisions by now. The reality is, we believe, that much of the protesting is ritualistic in nature, disguising satisfaction at the many positive and enjoyable features associated with a continual round of meetings. For one thing, if you're invited to many meetings, this must signify your importance in the organization (or at least you can imagine that it does). Certainly when people cease to be invited to meetings – even meetings which previously they deplored – they become extremely anxious, uncertain and insecure.

The other benefits (some listed here with a smidgeon of cynicism) are:

- At a meeting you are (relatively) immune from interruptions and other forms of time-wasting.
- If the meeting becomes tedious, you can switch off and so some serious thinking – this is less conspicuous than playing with your portable PC.
- Refreshments of a superior kind (real coffee and Bourbon biscuits) may be served at the meeting, and this is your only chance to take advantage of such small victories.

More seriously, let's now look at some of the reasons why meetings fail, why meetings are held, and what can be done to improve the effectiveness of meetings so far as time management is concerned.

WHY DO MEETINGS FAIL?

There are many answers to this question, some of them unprintable, but in essence we think there are seven principal reasons.

1. **The meeting is unnecessary.** When we come shortly to review the purposes of meetings, we may con-

clude that some of these objectives could be achieved without the necessity of a meeting at all. For example, if a meeting is held to dispense information, then this aim could be accomplished more efficiently by the simple distribution of a memo, notice or letter. If it is argued that a meeting enables the information to be explained and clarified, then telephone or computer-linked helpline and enquiry systems can enable these functions to be performed, again without the need for a meeting. After all, there are many situations in which large organizations – like banks, building societies and local authorities – must communicate information to their 'customers' in circumstances where meetings are simply not a practical option. If they can transmit their messages successfully (and furnish feedback procedures), the same processes could be readily adapted to the smaller information networks found in companies.

2. **The meeting isn't properly planned.** There may have been no advance briefing by the chairperson to ensure that everybody knows why they are there and what is to be accomplished. The agenda (assuming there is one, and it is distributed prior to the meeting itself) may include brief titles which do not adequately describe what is to be discussed, and therefore participants cannot prepare themselves adequately. Relevant supporting information is not supplied. On the other hand, even when an agenda is circulated beforehand, backed up by appropriate explanatory notes, members may still fail to do their homework. What's worse, they are allowed to get away with it, and so these inefficient practices continue.

3. **The environment is not appropriate.** The room or

space in which the meeting is held can be too large, too small, too hot, too cold, too noisy, overlooked from neighbouring offices or corridors. The meeting can be uncomfortable or enervatingly relaxed. Unscheduled interruptions may be condoned and even encouraged. External distractions (passing aircraft, parking cars, itinerant secretaries) prevent participants from concentrating on the business in hand. A long boardroom table inhibits eye contact; a round table maximizes participation but offers no obvious power position for the chairperson (or anybody else).

Perhaps the most dynamic meetings take place in rooms where there is no seating at all for the members. Because everyone has to stand, issues are resolved without delay or prevarication. The meeting generates an even greater sense of urgency if no refreshments are provided.

4. **The wrong people are present (and the right people are absent).** The presence of a RentaCrowd contingent means that the meeting includes items that do not interest all the members, or that decisions are made by people who are not responsible for the outcome. Equally, too many members may inhibit frank and free discussion; too few people will be unrepresentative.

5. **The chairperson (or leader) is inadequate.** Ideally, the leader's role is to keep the members on course and to remind them of the task in hand, whilst simultaneously creating and maintaining a supportive atmosphere in which people feel they can contribute if they wish. Control methods should steer a middle course between the kind of stylized rigidity which stifles debate, and the permissiveness which allows the discussion to stray into irrelevancies.

6. **Time management at the meeting is poor.** The meeting does not start on time, and appears to be open-ended because there is no scheduled finish-time. Perhaps because of uncertainty about the precise point at which the meeting will begin, some members arrive late – occasionally even the chair is late, too – and the onset of the meeting is postponed until what is perceived to be a quorum is present. If there is an agenda, it does not specify approximate time slots for each item. Individual members are allowed to repeat themselves and to monopolize the floor, leaving others silent, frustrated with futile anger.

7. **The objectives for the meeting are unclear.** This is the most significant cause of failure for meetings, because it may explain the uncertain approach adopted by the meeting's leader, the fact that some members are difficult to control (they have ambiguous guidelines), and the prevalence of talk about pet grievances 'owned' by some of the participants. In fact, of course, it is semantically inaccurate to talk about 'the objectives of the *meeting*' because the word 'meeting' is a descriptive term applicable to any gathering of two or more people *who themselves have objectives*: the 'meeting' is an inanimate phenomenon which cannot have separate objectives of its own. If it is true, then, that only the *individuals* at the meeting can have objectives, it follows that there is plenty of room for these objectives to differ. The leader may think, and even state, that 'the objective of this meeting is to agree on our proposed marketing strategy for 1994', but there may be others whose objectives will be quite different, declared or on some hidden agenda.

We must therefore go on now to look at the possible reasons why meetings take place. As in every aspect of time management, we can only allocate time efficiently if we know what we are trying to achieve.

THE OBJECTIVES FOR MEETINGS

In our experience, meetings, conferences and discussions are held for one or more of the following reasons. These reasons can also be applied to the presence of individual agenda items for meetings of a more discursive nature (e.g., monthly sales team meetings which can embrace a variety of purposes: communications, collective decision-making, creative thinking and changing attitudes).

1. **To communicate information.** Because it is normally more efficient to distribute information in written form, the information-dispensing meeting may take place because it is important – for status reasons or to improve co-ordination – that everyone receives the information simultaneously. Further, if information is transmitted at a meeting, the details can be clarified and the ambiguities removed there and then.

   With the *prepared* information-dispensing meeting, participants get the information in advance and the meeting is used to reinforce the message, answer queries and (if necessary) defend management action. This contrasts with *emergency* information-dispensing meetings, called at short notice to keep people up to date with a rapidly developing situation. Such meetings include those called by large organizations (and often held simultaneously in various locations) in order to announce significant redundancies or business closures.

An important feature of the information-dispensing meeting is that control is firmly centralized through the chairperson, who may do most of the talking.

2. **To elicit information from the members.** This type of meeting occurs where, for instance, a sales manager wants to update himself on the progress being made by a new product, and therefore seeks feedback from his assembled sales representatives. Whether or not this type of meeting is successful depends on the atmosphere of open discussion and the willingness of the group to engage in a free exchange of views. Will it be acceptable for a sales representative openly to admit that the new product is a disaster?

3. **To elicit information from one person which has possible value for the group as a whole.** Examples include a briefing by the marketing manager for members of a regional sales team, or a contribution from one individual who has specialized knowledge and experience.

4. **To throw up creative ideas.** The process of generating ideas in a group, commonly known as brainstorming, relies on the assumption that the flow of ideas will be stimulated once members of the group can be persuaded to throw away their inhibitions. To put it another way, 'left-brain' thinking (logical, rational, systematic and 'sensible') has to be replaced by 'right-brain' thinking (creative, intuitive, playful and 'childish'). This can be achieved if certain simple rules are followed:

- The group size does not exceed eight or nine participants.
- The leader initially states the problem by writing it

on the flipchart with the formulation 'In how many ways can we . . . ?' (Example: 'In how many ways can we reduce our overheads?')

- The group is invited to offer restatements of the problem, in order to secure maximum 'ownership' of the issue among the majority of the participants. Alternative restatements could include 'In how many ways can we cut staff?' or 'In how many ways can we increase sales?' or 'In how many ways can we spend less on petrol?'

- One of the restatements, or the original statement, is selected for eventual brainstorming, with the consent of the group.

- The leader introduces a brief 'warm-up' exercise in order to assist the transition into 'right-brain' thinking. This is especially necessary if the brainstorming phase follows a sequence of agenda items which have required 'left-brain' analysis and logical treatment. Examples of 'warm-up' exercises include asking the group to think of possible uses for a paper clip, handkerchief, matchbox, house-brick or tin of shoe polish.

- During the subsequent brainstorming session itself, the leader acts as a facilitator, writing every idea on flipchart sheets. It is essential that every idea is greeted positively, no matter how absurd it seems to be, because the whole purpose of the exercise is to simulate a large *quantity* of ideas (their *quality* can be scrutinized later).

5. **To reach decisions.** At a meeting of this type, the leader (or whoever 'owns' the problem) will outline the situation, invite decision alternatives, evaluate them, and move towards the consensus of a final choice.

6. **To make decisions.** Here, by contrast, the decision choices have been identified *before* the meeting: the group simply has to select one of the options. Thus most debates in the House of Commons, if they can be classified as 'meetings' at all, are *decision-making* meetings because the members are voting on their preferences about a range of pre-selected alternatives.

7. **To air grievances and reveal attitudes.** Such meetings can occasionally be useful in allowing a catharis (purging of the emotions) to take place, even if the chairperson/leader can do little to remove the causes of any dissatisfaction. Normally a meeting would not be held with the sole or principal purpose of encouraging participants to air their grievances, but allowing people to express their emotions may be an essential prelude to more reasoned discussions on other topics.

8. **To change behaviour and attitudes.** In this category fall the more stage-managed meetings called to promote Total Quality Management on a company-wide basis, or small-scale quality-improvement groups held among department or section staff.

As already stated at the outset, any given meeting may have different objectives at various moments of its existence. One agenda item may call for creative brain-storming, while another is of the information-dispensing type. Such variations call for sensitive handling by the chairperson and flexibility on the part of members.

WHAT CAN YOU DO TO MANAGE TIME EFFECTIVELY AT MEETINGS?

1. Prepare yourself thoroughly.
- What is your overall objective? What are your objectives for the various stages of the meeting?
- Outline a plan for the meeting with your opening words; try to predict what is likely to happen (especially what objections and difficulties you are likely to encounter) and prepare for it.
- Organize visual aids and equipment, if appropriate.
- Arrange the accommodation, bearing in mind the need to maximize eye contact between yourself (as the leader) and the individual members. A circular table will encourage participation, but a rectangular table will give you more control: which is appropriate for your purpose?
- Make notes for reference at the meeting itself.

2. Structure the agenda.
- Circulate a Notice about the meeting [see the specimen proformas at the end of this chapter] inviting items for the Agenda. Not only will this give you some advance warning about the issues on other people's minds, but it will give you the authority you need for disallowing 'Any Other Business' requests on the grounds that these items could (and should) have been incorporated into the Agenda.
- When putting together the Agenda itself, make sure that the topics are arranged in a logical, sensible sequence, with connecting items linked together.
- All Agenda headings should be stated in such a way that the members know the *purpose* behind the topic. Thus 'Management of the Staff Restaurant' is not good enough: the issue needs to be clarified,

maybe along the lines of 'Management of the Staff Restaurant: Need to Make Decisions in view of the Resignation of our existing Caterers.'

- Allocate rough timings for each Agenda topic, and give precise start and finish times for the meeting as a whole [again, see the specimen proforma for an Agenda accompanying this chapter]. Ideally, the finish time should be phrased as 'Finish *by* . . .' because there is always a possibility that the Agenda can be completed earlier than the planned deadline.

- The chances of this happening are increased if you deliberately schedule the meeting so that its finish coincides with some other event that imposes time pressures on your participants. Meetings held on Friday afternoons are frequently more incisive because members are beginning to think about the weekend, especially if they are also conscious of the long and arduous drive home. Meetings starting an hour or so before lunch are typically more disciplined than those where a 9 a.m. opening subliminally persuades people that, in effect, they have blocked off the whole half-day for the event.

- Distribute the Agenda well in advance (at least three working days before the meeting), together with any informational background documents. It is a waste of time to communicate facts by dispensing them orally or by distributing papers at the meeting itself.

- Make it clear, in the formulation of the Agenda, that you do not intend to allow 'Any Other Business' items, on the grounds that they do not allow adequate thought in advance by the members, and so AOB decisions tend to be ill-conceived. Further, the raising of 'Any Other Business' is often a reflection of sheer laziness among people who could have put the topic on the Agenda but couldn't raise the energy to do so. Sometimes, too, 'Any Other Business' is manipulated for machiavellian purposes by individuals who deliberately try to get decisions agreed without allowing participants to think about the implications carefully (which they would be able to do if they'd had advance warning within the Agenda).

- A further danger about 'Any Other Business' is that typically it appears at the end of the meeting. If you (as leader) want to send your team away with uplifted attitudes and renewed enthusiasm, your aim will almost certainly be scuppered because of the negative thinking, defeatist opinions and all-round depression encouraged by the expression of AOB complaints and grievances.

- If you really feel you *must* allow an 'Any Other Business' component into your meeting – specifically for any issues (fortunately rare) which are both Urgent and Unimportant in your prioritization system, then slot it in for a scheduled 10 minutes at the *beginning* of your meeting. Don't be embarrassed about refusing to accept a proposed AOB topic, either, on the possible grounds that:

  (a) It isn't *Urgent* and therefore doesn't require our immediate attention.

  (b) It is *Important* and therefore must be allocated more than ten minutes. Furthermore, it is essential that we all have the chance to think about it in advance, because of its (actual or potential) significance.

  (c) It isn't *Urgent* and it isn't *Important*, so it doesn't deserve any time at all.

3. Starting the meeting

- Open the meeting *exactly* at the advertised time, even if some people haven't arrived. You should start on the dot even if you're the only person in the room and you therefore spend a few moments talking to yourself. Your members will soon learn that it is your practice to start on time, and will make sure they are there in future (especially if their early absence means that their names appear in the 'Action By' column of the Minutes).

- Begin by clarifying the purpose and scope of the meeting, and the ground rules. These should not be up for debate, otherwise you will get some nit-pickers who will want to discuss procedure all day, aided and abetted by others who see an opportunity to 'talk out' some of the later agenda items.

4. Controlling the progress of the meeting.

- Discourage personal arguments, but note their relevance to the group dynamics and to the positions taken by certain individuals when ostensibly unrelated issues are being pursued.

- Encourage participation from reticent members, by posing direct questions to them ('What do you feel about this?')

- Curtail contributions by talkative members, by intervening when they pause to draw breath ('That's an excellent point, Bill; now let's hear from . . .'), by holding up your hand in front of the rambler's face, or by posing questions to them in negative form ('You don't have anything to add, do you?')

- Summarize progress from time to time, clarifying points of agreement and disagreement.

- Ensure that your initial timing plans (for managing the agenda) are broadly achieved.

- Be sensitive to non-verbal signals and body language from members (that's why it is important to have a seating pattern which permits maximum eye contact round the group), especially indications of impatience with a prolonged discussion.

5. Closing the meeting.

- Make sure that everyone knows what has been agreed, who is responsible for implementation, and that any deadlines are spelled out, with unequivocal acceptance by those involved.
- Be tolerant of minority views or those whose opinions and preferences have been rejected. It may be worthwhile to pass them a consoling word after the meeting itself, and could even save a lot of time in the future, if it helps to reduce resentment and remove the impetus for revenge.
- End the meeting *precisely* at the advertised time, or sooner. As with starting the meeting on time, it will help your reputation for efficiency. If you finish earlier than the target time, people will believe you must have supernatural powers and your charisma will go before you like a beacon.

6. After the Meeting.

- For most management meetings, the only document which requires subsequent circulation is an **Action Note**, specifying what is to happen as a result of the meeting, who is to do it, and by when (usually, the date and time of the next meeting).
- **Action Notes** should be circulated within 24 hours: this is easily achieved if you use a standard proforma (suitably adapted for your specific organization) like that supplied at the end of this chapter.

7. If you are only a member of the meeting . . .

- You still have a responsibility for ensuring that the time is spent productively. If you waste your time at a meeting, it is unreasonable to place the blame entirely on the chairperson, without asking yourself what *you* could have done in terms of constructive interventions.

- If other participants are garrulous, emotional or wandering into irrelevance, you don't have to simply sit there doodling, playing with your calculator or exchanging cynical glances with other members who think like you do.

- What you *can* do is suggest supportive phrases like 'What I think John is trying to say is . . .' or 'I can see Bill's point of view . . .' and then steer the discussion back to its prescribed theme.

- If the chairperson is not very efficient, equally you can help to push the meeting along, *not* by a frontal attack on the individual's competence (which will only raise the emotional temperature and may be politically unwise if the chairperson is senior to you) but by interventions like 'I wonder whether we could hear from Ted on this point, as I know he's been doing some work on it' or 'Would you like me to summarize where we've got to on this topic?'

- The important and even essential principle of participation at meetings is that you speak in a calm, moderate, positive and constructive fashion. There is no advantage in deliberately raising the emotional heat in the group (except in highly unusual circumstances): the display of emotion and the subsequent return to 'normal' discussion is itself a manifestation of wasted time.

HELPING WITH THE PAPERWORK

On the next three pages are specimen proformas for inviting agenda topics, the Agenda itself and the post-meeting Action Notes. We have found these worthwhile and effective: it is a simple matter to print similar versions for your own use, perhaps incorporating changes relevant to your own role and the needs of your specific organization. Once you have a stock of these proformas, suitably adapted, then it takes little time to insert the contents, even in handwriting, if you don't have immediate access to a word processor.

NOTICE

CHAIRMAN:	NOTICE OF A MEETING OF THE:
SECRETARY:	TO BE HELD ON: _____ 19 __
MEMBERS:	BEGINNING AT: ....
	ENDING AT: ....
	VENUE:

If you have any items for the Agenda of the above meeting please notify them in the space below and return this notice to the Secretary by _____ 19 ____. It would help members at the meeting if you would attach notes or documents that explain the issue you wish to be on the Agenda.

ITEMS FOR THE AGENDA

DATE: ....

FROM: ....

AGENDA

CHAIRMAN:	AGENDA FOR A MEETING OF THE:
SECRETARY:	TO BE HELD ON: _____ 19____
MEMBERS:	BEGINNING AT:
	ENDING AT:
	VENUE:

ITEM NO.	AGENDA	TIMING

APOLOGIES TO CHAIRMAN OR SECRETARY BEFORE THE MEETING PLEASE

ACTION NOTE

PRESENT:	MEETING OF THE:		19 ___
APOLOGIES:	HELD ON		
OTHER MEMBERS:			

ITEM NO	ACTION	ACTION BY (Name)	DEADLINE

CHAPTER 10

The Links Between Stress and Poor Time Management

WHAT IS STRESS AND WHY DISCUSS IT IN A BOOK ABOUT TIME MANGEMENT?

Certainly there is no agreed definition of what constitutes 'stress'. The basic idea is very simple: there are forces, pressures, constraints and demands which act on individuals. If some people cannot cope with or control these pressures, then there is the possibility that they can suffer damage. The damage may be psychological or physiological, or even both; the causes are often attributed to the generic phenomenon of 'stress', when in fact it is clear that the *real* causes are to be found in the events which trigger the symptoms of 'stress'.

Stress, particularly 'executive stress', has become a very fashionable topic for discussion among managers in the past few years. The reasons are twofold:

1. The pace of managerial life has undoubtedly quickened, with individuals being asked to perform more and more responsibilities without any of their previous accountabilities being taken away from them. There is a growing focus on performance and results, with awesome penalties for failure. The constant

emphasis on innovation and change is a particular threat for managers accustomed to a somewhat leisurely existence, especially in 'softer' hierarchies like the Civil Service, local government and the public sector generally.

2. Managers themselves are flattered by the notion that they might be susceptible to a condition which is all their own. They are even more flattered if they think they are surviving the rigours of the disease without permanent or irreparable harm.

In reality, it is worth noting almost as an aside that 'executive stress' is little more than a myth. There is no evidence that the rigours of technological change and performance pressures hit at managers and white-collar staff any more than at blue-collar workers. Indeed, the evidence suggests rather the opposite, despite the fact that clerical employees have suffered particularly vitriolic shake-outs in the recession of the early 1990s. If there were thought to be any connection between the incidence of stress and shortened life-expectancy, then again the figures do not support the view that 'executives' are particularly prone to an early death compared with their manually-employed counterparts. On the contrary, life expectancy is positively correlated with hierarchical position: the more senior you are, the more likely it is that you will live a long time.

Nonetheless, there is sufficient *real* stress about for us to regard it as a serious problem, and we certainly think it warrants a chapter to itself in this book.

The first thing to say is that in the context of time management, we are not concerned with occasional bursts of stress which occur (for example) when you just manage to avoid a lethal collision on the motorway. This is not to say that such bursts are harmless. When we are confronted with a sudden threat to our survival, then our bodies react instantly by sending out a surge of adrenalin, preparing us (as once similar urges did to primitive man) for 'Fight' or 'Flight'. We are either going to attack the threat to our survival, or run away from it. Normally either of these behaviours would be very sensible reactions if the threat were to be, say, a night-time burglar, a fire in the building or the appearance of a sabre-toothed tiger. However, the trouble with many of the 'stressors' (stress-provoking incidents) in modern society is that they occur in circumstances which make it virtually impossible for us to choose either of the 'Fight' or 'Flight' options. If you have just managed to brake in time to avoid a motorway crash, you are under stress, you have adrenalin coursing through your body, but what can you do? You have nothing concrete to fight, and you certainly can't run away. It is this inability to act, to respond, to do something which the adrenalin has made us ready to do, which is damaging to the heart and the blood pressure.

We have to live with such occasional stress, cope with it if possible, and control our reactions if we can. If one-off 'stressors' are harmful, however, then long-term stress is even more dangerous. Such stress is recognizable in any of the following ways (depending on the individual):

- *General features*: persistent negative changes in psychological functioning.
- *Mood changes*: irritability, resentment, panic feelings, anxiety, guilt, depression.
- *Cognitive changes*: trouble in concentrating, difficulty in making decisions and 'switching off'.
- *Behavioural changes*: making errors, double-checking everything, use of palliatives (drugs,

144

tranquillisers, tobacco, coffee, sleeping pills, worry beads).
- *Secondary physical symptoms*: disturbed sleep, headaches, chest pains, dizziness.

The causes of stress (to be discussed in the next section) do not necessarily include poor time management, but the *consequence* of stress invariably mean poor time management. The individual is pre-occupied, repetitious, disturbed, incapable of acting rationally, self-absorbed, temporarily absent from work and inattentive. Thus the situation typically deteriorates. The original stress breeds ineffective time management, which in turn generates further stress, and so on. So stress is relevant to time management, as possible cause and certain effect.

WHAT ARE THE CAUSES OF STRESS?

There is no singe event in anyone's life which is *guaranteed* to produce stress. The Washington University survey of 5000 Americans concluded that 'Death of spouse' is normally the most stressful occurrence we encounter: accordingly they give it a 'Stress Index' of 100, with other (less significant) events spiralling downwards as shown in the following table of specimen incidents:

Death of spouse	100
Divorce	73
Prison term	63
Personal injury/illness	53
Marriage	50
Fired from work	47
Marital reconciliation	45

Retirement	45
Sexual difficulties	39
Change to different job	36
Change in work responsibilities	29
Daughter/son leaving home	29
Outstanding personal achievement	28
Wife begins/stops work	26
Trouble with boss	23
Change in work conditions/hours	20
Holidays	13
Christmas	12

Although this study covered a large sample, its figures conceal a wide range of variations. For some, 'Death of spouse' would not be a particularly stressful experience, whereas for others 'Christmas' is a blood-curdling nightmare.

It is often claimed, in fact, that **one person's stress is another's challenge.** Something is viewed as stressful to an individual only if he or she perceives it as such; whether they view it as stressful is likely to depend on whether they think they can 'cope' with it. In 1973 another American survey, this time of 3000 people, asked its respondents to identify their greatest fear. Although the customary answers were given – fear of heights, flying, spiders and enclosed spaces – the greatest fear of all (expressed by 41 per cent) was the fear of speaking in front of a group. By contrast, only 19 per cent admitted to a fear of death. So it seems that standing up to deliver a presentation is a terrifying scenario for many people – and yet there are some who thrive on it and would be seriously deprived if the opportunity to harangue were taken away from them.

Two other features are notable about the causes of stress, and both are suggested by the Washington University survey:

- Many stressful events in our lives are meant to be enjoyable (marriage, holidays, Christmas, retirement) and yet are often associated with anxiety.
- Work-related causes are somewhat less significant as 'stressors' than personal experiences (though this is somewhat contradicted by BUPA's 1992 Stress Survey in the UK, which placed work and financial problems firmly at the top of the list.

So far as time management is concerned, the most significant 'stressors' are those connected with work and employment. If you're under stress now, or think you might become stressed, then to prevent or mitigate the situation you have first to understand where the stress is coming from. Here are some possibilities:

- **Working conditions.** In particular, there is evidence that poor mental health is related to tasks of a repetitive, short-job-cycle kind, using few skills and requiring little involvement from the employee. Excessive hours or an unpleasant work environment can also be significant for some types of work.
- **Work overload.** This can be either *quantitative* (too much to do) or *qualitative* (the task is too difficult), or both. Work overload is especially common among employees in the 1990s; it is clearly linked to time-control disciplines and the selection of priorities.
- **Role Ambiguity.** Tension occurs when an individual lacks sufficient information about the scope and responsibilities of his job, the key tasks, the defined objectives, and the expectations entertained by others (colleagues, customers, seniors) about acceptable standards of performance.
- **Role Conflict.** Sometimes individuals are torn by conflicting job demands, by doing things they don't

really want to do and don't regard themselves as capable of doing. Role conflict is especially common among those who have both designated 'line' responsibilities and also project-team duties: when there is a struggle between the demands of each obligation, which should take precedence? Role conflict also occurs when managers leading internal service functions (like a marketing information department) have various 'customers' beating on their door simultaneously.

- **Relationships at work: The Boss.** When a boss is perceived as 'considerate', there is more likely to be a relationship of mutual trust and respect. By contrast, employees can rapidly exhibit stress if the boss does not give them performance feedback in a helpful and constructive way.
- **Relationships at work: Subordinates.** Increasingly managers are learning to manage by participation and two-way consultation; for some this is a considerable source of resentment, anxiety and stress. Such managers may not only feel sensitive about the perceived erosion of their former powers, but may also be subjected to apparently contradictory pressures towards more participation *and* high production: they may believe that it is impossible to have both. In addition, of course, some subordinates may be uncooperative, unpleasant or inadequate; these symptoms may be 'stressors' for the manager who does not know how to confront such situations.
- **Relationshps at work: Colleagues.** Apart from the obvious factors associated with interpersonal rivalries and so forth, stress can also be induced by a lack of adequate social support in different situations – in other words, by the isolation of being a senior manager and having few people in whom one can confide.

- **Career Development.** Two major clusters of causal elements can be identified in this area:
  1. Lack of job security, fear of redundancy, obsolescence or early retirement.
  2. Status incongruity (under-promotion or over-promotion) and frustration at having reached a perceived career ceiling, especially applicable to 'plateaued' managers in today's flattened hierarchies.
- **Organizational Structure and Climate.** The causes of stress here focus on such elements as a feeling of little or no participation in the decision-making process, no sense of belonging, lack of effective consultation and communication, restrictions on behaviour (e.g., through budgets) and the impact of office politics. The situation is especially stressful when organizations undergo a period of rapid cultural change, perhaps spearheaded by a newly-appointed chief executive. Some managers further down the hierarchy are bound to find such change unpalatable and may react with various kinds of physical and psychological symptoms.

WHAT CAN YOU DO TO MANAGE STRESS SUCCESSFULLY?

Clearly you cannot create an environment which is entirely stress-free – nor would it be desirable to do so, even if it were possible, because our brains thrive when confronted by a controllable range of stimuli. (Sensory deprivation is close to being a stress-free environment, in a sense, but it is very definitely a powerful source of stress to those who experience it – which is what it is so successful as a method of interrogation.) So the issue is not one of eliminating the 'stressors', but rather concerns the development of preventative strategies (for ensuring that events, which in themselves are neutral, do not become 'stressors' for us) and coping mechanisms (for keeping our stress levels under control). You may find that some of the following techniques will ring bells for you, either because you can use them immediately or can adapt them for your specific (unique) needs.

- **Work Overload.** In many cases, although people above you in the hierarchy may be directly responsible for the allocation of tasks (and the imposition of deadlines associated with their completion), you have some scope for negotiation if you're prepared to use it. In practice, many people at work are frightened to admit that they can't do a job within the time limit specified: this sets a self-fulfilling feedback loop into operation where management continues to think that the job can be done, and organizes future work schedules accordingly. To escape from such vicious circles, initiative from the stressed individual is essential, taking the form of an approach to the boss in order to discuss the situation. It is important to supply concrete evidence to bolster the case; your negotiating objectives can include some postponement of target dates and/or clear allocation of priorities if time pressures don't permit all your tasks to be accomplished.

- **Work Underload.** This is a 'stressor' not only because you are bored and unproductive, but also because you are likely to feel unimportant and inadequate. In such cases, you must first do some reality-testing by checking with the boss about the reasons for the work shortfall, how long the situation is likely to persist, and whether there is any prospect of increased activity. If it is true that you are being deprived of work because of your (perceived) incompetence, then this issue is probably better confronted than left to fester. On the other hand, the reality-testing overture may provide positive feedback to management that you have spare capacity. An even better strategy is to generate your ideas for worthwhile, value-added assignments and seek their adoption and sponsorship from above.

- **Role Ambiguity and Role Conflict.** In either of these scenarios, the first thing to do is to approach the person responsible for defining your role (usually your immediate boss) and discuss the issue, asking for a more clear-cut agreement and understanding about what is required from you.

  Secondly, the boss should be encouraged to provide four separate lists of what he thinks
  (a) You should do more of
  (b) You could do better at
  (c) You should do less of (or stop altogether) and
  (d) You should keep on doing or maintain unchanged

  If you don't feel confident about extracting these lists from your boss, then produce them yourself and pass them to him for comment. At the same time, it would be helpful if you generated your own list of things that you think the boss should do more of, less of, and so forth.

  After the lists have been exchanged, there should be a process of discussion and negotiation, eventually leading to a 'deal' between boss and subordinate ('If you do X, I will do Y').

- **Personal Relationships at Risk.** These stress-inducing situations are potentially the most difficult to handle. Much can often be achieved by a direct yet friendly approach to the other person, seeking an opportunity to discuss differences with a view to understanding each other's position more clearly. Alternatively, it may be necessary to avoid contacts which are likely to be provocative and inflammatory.

- **Career Planning.** If uncertainty over your career prospects is a relevant issue in your case, then you should make a determined effort to acquire as much *accurate* (as opposed to over-optimistic) information as possible about the situation. This is easier said than done, of course, especially if your organization is undergoing rapid strategic change, or is suffering in the throes of what is euphemistically known as 'down-sizing', or is flattening its hierarchy as part of an empowerment programme. Indeed, one of the consequences of such fashionable development in the 1990s is the emergence of a large breed of 'plateaued managers' with up to 20 or 30 years of employment ahead of them but negligible chances for further advancement. What are the options? One choice is to adjust your personal goals to fit in with the reality; another (possibly linked) is to focus on goals outside the organization altogether; a third course is to seek lateral moves and breadth of experience, in order to sustain your desire for constant challenge (and also, conceivably, to open up additional avenues of escape from your corporate blockage).

Type A and Type B Behaviour Patterns
In 1968, Friedman and Rosenman's book, *Type A Behaviour and Your Heart*, argued that heart disease is a consequence not so much of factors like smoking, lack of exercise and cholesterol, but is rather associated with

the fundamental lifestyle characteristics of the Type A person:

- Intense drive and aggression
- Ambition and competitiveness
- Constant pressure to get things done
- Sense of urgency
- Decisiveness
- Speaks fast but uses few words
- Always on time or early
- 'Polyphasic thinker' (capable of thinking about several things simultaneously)
- Schedules more in less time

The Type A individual tends to be much valued in middle management for many organizations. Yet, according to Rosenman and Friedman:

- *The Type A person is twice as prone to the onset of clinical heart disease*
- *The Type A person is five times more prone to a second heart attack*
- *The Type A person is twice as prone to fatal heart attacks*

Or, to put it another way: from the viewpoint of the Type A manager, **death is Nature's way of telling you to slow down.** Type A people don't typically make it to the top in large organizations, partly because a Darwinian process of natural selection weeds them out before they have any chance of getting there. Moreover, Type A qualities may be desirable in middle management, but are less valuable for senior mangement roles where strategic wisdom becomes preferable to rapid response. So people recovering from heart attacks, or those with warning signs, are counselled (in effect) to manage their time more effectively and join the Type B brigade: relaxed, uncompetitive, laid back, leisurely, self-controlled, the sequential thinker, a calm person with a calming influence on others.

If you see yourself as a Type A manager, or with Type A tendencies, then it does make sense to try some of the Friedman and Rosenman recipes for moving towards a Type B model:

- **Try to restrain yourself from being the centre of attention** – learn, for example, to keep silent at meetings, initially for two or three minutes at a stretch, and then for longer as you get used to it.
- **Become aware of your obsessional time-directed life and change your patterns of behaviour** – the results of a Time Activity Analysis should highlight the principal causes of your problem, e.g., your reluctance to delegate or your unassailable belief in your personal indispensability. Removing the fax machine from your bedside table would be a start.
- **Review the causes of your 'hurry sickness'** – it's probable that you're either not prioritizing at all (and therefore assume that *everything* is top priority) or that you're failing to discriminate adequately between the things which are genuinely Important/Urgent and those which are not.
- **Create some outside interests** – but make sure they aren't competitive, because you'll simply import your Type A lifestyle into your world of leisure. Squash is very popular among Type A people because (a) it is intensely competitive, and (b) you can compress a lot of exercise into a limited time-window. To unwind, Type A managers should take up activities like brass-rubbing, stamp-collecting, yoga or reading Proust's

À La Recherche du Temps Perdu.

- **Don't make unnecessary appointments and un-achievable deadlines** – stop rushing off to an endless succession of meetings (send someone else to at least half of them), be more discriminating about the people you see on a face-to-face basis (maybe a letter, memo, phone call or fax will do instead), set realistic targets.

- **Learn to say 'No'** – after you've tried it once or twice (in front of the mirror if necessary), you'll find it easy – and it works.

- **Take some stress-free 'breathing spaces' during the day** – don't schedule meetings and appointments for every available moment. Breathing spaces can be useful as a means of catching up with your commitments if anything overruns: it invariably generates stress in yourself and in others if your time-keeping becomes progressively worse as each day goes on. Even when earlier engagements have kept to time, a breathing space helps you do some thinking to prepare for the next round; you can recharge your psychic batteries and you may even try a bit of aimless MBWA.

Good News for Type A People: The Concept of 'Control'

Type A people typically strive for control over their environment. It may be, therefore, that the Type A person creates his own stress, during a period of rapid change, through desperate efforts to remain 'in charge'. The need for challenge is certainly an important element in the well-being of Type A managers, and they often deliberately select a lifestyle which incorporates such challenges. In short then, we have two categories of Type A individuals:

(1) Those who are Type A because they **want** to be – the seekers after challenge.

(2) Those who are Type A because they **have** to be – in a desperate effort to remain 'in charge'.

Possibly this slightly more sophisticated classification helps to explain the fact that the relationship between Type A behaviour and coronary heart disease is more complex than was first imagined. It appears in practice that **Type A survivors actually outnumber Type B survivors in the longer term.** Several authorities think that this is because individuals who are *internally-oriented* (i.e., they believe they are controllers of their own destiny) engage in more adaptive health responses, both at preventative and remedial levels. Literally speaking, they *manage* their time rather than let time manage them. For this group, Type A behaviour is not associated with coronary-proneness.

A great deal of the current research into stress concentrates on the notion of *control*, which Taylor and Cooper define as '*a generalized expectancy concerning the extent to which an individual believes that reinforcement, rewards or success are either internally or externally controlled*'.

- An **internal** locus of control implies a belief in personal power and the ability to influence the outcome of events.

- An **external** locus of control implies the belief that personal power has a minimal effect on the outcome of events; more important elements are fate, chance or 'powerful others'.

People in managerial and professional positions tend to be more 'internally' oriented. However, the significance of the 'locus-of-control' perception seems to be especially important, so far as stress and health are concerned, for those individuals in positions characterized by role ambiguity.

Linking Type A and Type B characteristics on the one hand, and 'locus-of-control' perceptions on the other, we now have four groups of people:

1. **Charismatic** (*Type A and internal locus of control*): healthy, expressive, dominant, fast-moving, coping well and sociable. These individuals have *self-imposed* challenges, pressures and deadlines; they find these phenomena exciting and exhilarating; without them they would be stultified.

2. **Hostile** (*Type A and external locus of control*): competitive, expressive and dominant, but in a threatened, negative sense. People in this category are certainly fast-moving, but in their case it is because they sense they are in the grip of dynamic forces and a speed of change which, if these individuals were to slow down for a moment, would engulf them. They are victims of (time and work-imposed) pressure, not masters of it. As a result they are more coronary-prone.

3. **Relaxed** (*Type B and internal locus of control*): quiet, unexpressive, somewhat submissive, content. This group is probably less inclined to coronary heart disease because it comprises people who remain genuinely detached and emotionally separated from events which would, for others, constitute sources of anxiety and tension.

4. **Tense** (*Type B and external locus of control*): over-controlled, seeming unexpressive and inhibited, but liable to explode under sufficient challenge. These individuals *appear* to be detached, but inside

themselves they are seething with anger, hostility, aggression and (because their feelings have been ruthlessly suppressed) frustration. Such individuals can suffer the consequences in terms of psychological maturity and physical ill-health.

Classification into one of these four categories is not merely, or even principally, a matter of genes, heredity, socialization and temperament. Learning the skills of time management – especially those linked with assertiveness behaviour – can be an important aid to physical survival as well as a route to increased job satisfaction and career advancement. This is particularly true if the individual's self-help programme (towards a belief in the internal locus of control, coupled with physical fitness) is reinforced by appropriate processes supplied in enlightened organizations:

1. **Communication:** the evidence suggests that good communications (both upwards and downwards) help to reduce stress and increase job satisfaction.
2. **Control:** people gain a greater perception of their ability to control their time (and therefore their stress levels) as a result of reduced uncertainty and greater understanding of change forces and policies.
3. **Counselling:** where organizations provide counselling services, they help to offset the feeling that stress is a stigma. Counselling is even more effective when coupled with 'wellness' programmes like dietary and exercise advice.

CHAPTER 11

Pulling the Threads Together: The Self-Analysis Exercise in Time Management

INTRODUCTION

Most people claim they know where the time goes. But in fact they have only the haziest idea. Almost invariably there is a significant difference between claim and reality, a difference which is made painfully obvious once they have carried out a comprehensive investigation into where the time actually goes. The results of this investigation are frequently embarrassing, partly because they show how capable people are of deluding themselves, and partly because of revelations about time-wasting, dissipated energies, unproductive and fragmented activities, procrastination, interruptions and the absence of any value-added dimension.

If you seriously intend to improve your own time management, you must start from where you are, which means you must analyse what you are currently doing. The following exercise will equip you with the basic

159

data and then point you in the right direction – the direction appropriate for your particular needs.

INSTRUCTIONS

- Keep a record of how you spend your time over five representative days (which need not be consecutive), using the Activity Record on page 185. Select any five days which look to you as if they might be 'typical'; don't choose days when you're working at home (if you don't normally do that) or when you'll be totally occupied with a tour of inspection from your Managing Director.
- If you have a very fragmented day, with many short-term events and interruptions, it may be necessary to take a 'snapshot' note of what you are doing at 15-minute intervals. You will need to activate an electronic timer of some sort to remind you of each 15-minute point, and then you must write down what you are doing when the buzzer sounds.
- Preferably, however, you should keep an accurate and comprehensive record of *everything* you do throughout the time you are at work.
- If your normal routine encompasses shift work or unconventional hours, then the Activity Record proforma must be modified to suit your situation. Don't forget, however, that the Activity Record should incorporate time spent on work issues when travelling to and from home, and while at home.
- In our experience, making an accurate record of your activities will prove very difficult. This is not so much because the act of writing everything down becomes painful and laborious, but rather because *many people lie and cheat, even to themselves.*

Putting down the telephone after a private call, you may 'forget' to note it on your Activity Record; returning to your workstation after 15 minutes in the lavatory reading the paper, you may 'estimate' that in fact you have been away for only five minutes. Managers have been known to elongate their working hours so that they appear to be workaholics, or conversely to reduce them artificially to more 'reasonable' proportions. Obviously, if you succumb to any of these tempting distortions, the data you collect will be misleading (at best) and the exercise will become futile. Remember that the only person who is going to see the information is you – it can be destroyed once you've acted on it – and therefore **falsification is pointless**.

- If you have a secretary, or a subordinate who temporarily has little to do, or a work-experience trainee, then you may be able to persuade them to keep your Activity Record for you. They will have to follow you around constantly with a clipboard, of course, but at least their observations will be slightly more objective.

HOW TO ANALYSE THE RESULTS

Your Activity Record will not be much use unless you make sense of the results. To do this effectively, you must group your activities into recognizably different activities, and then make judgements about which kinds of activity are more profitable and advantageous than others.

Here are three possible modes of analysis. You will probably find that one of them will be more productive than the others, but much depends on your precise role and the kind of organization in which you work. Classifying your activities from your chosen five days against any one of these category-systems, however, is almost certainly going to throw up pointers to the more effective time management of time.

For some activities, precise allocation into one category or another may prove difficult. We have tried to be as helpful as possible in explaining the categories, and in giving examples, but clearly we cannot be comprehensive. In the end you must make a choice about where you put a specific activity, and having made that choice you must stick to it in the sense that all other similar activities should be similarly classified. It is vital, of course, that you don't double-count any particular activity.

You may even find that the categories we suggest aren't sufficiently all-embracing to address every aspect of your current role. If so, then by all means generate additional categories, so long as you try your best to group similar activities together. If you create too many categories, you'll find that it's hard to separate the wood from the trees.

Mode 1: The Value-Added Analysis
This classification uses the model around which this book is constructed. According to our approach, your role (and therefore your activity pattern) has four dimensions:

(1) **Maintenance:** fire-fighting, the resolution of 'crises' and handling everyday operational difficulties. Examples include the process of filling a vacancy, preparing next year's budgets, counselling staff with personal problems, filling in routine returns.

(2) **Crisis Prevention:** making sure that previous 'crises'

don't recur, or that predictable future 'crises' can be contained (either through prevention or mitigation). Examples include: parts of the performance review process (concerned with rectifying earlier performance difficulties), proactive contingency planning and time spent on the development of policies/systems/routines.

(3) **Performance Improvement:** finding ways to perform your current role **better** (to a higher standard of quality), **faster** (with results delivered sooner without any loss of quality) and **cheaper** (fewer calls on resources like hardware, software and people). Examples include time spent on quality-improvement programmes and activities, brainstorming with your team, thinking and planning.

(4) **Change Management:** introducing new ideas, new ways of doing things, new products and services, new ways of organizing. Examples include networking both inside and outside the organization, the pilot-testing of new products and services with 'customers', the authorship and circulation of proposals for change, attendance at future-oriented conferences and perusal of strategically-relevant literature.

As we've already emphasized earlier in the books, the first two of these roles, *Maintenance* and *Crisis Prevention*, do not add value and the proportion of your time that you spend on them is a reflection of your personal *efficiency* (not effectiveness). You add value to your organization by the extent to which you focus on *Performance Improvement* and *Change Management*: the larger the amount of time you devote to these processes, the more *effective* you are (potentially).

If your Activity Record shows that you spend virtually no time at all on *Performance Improvement* and

Change Management, you are in serious danger. Your senior managers may wonder why they employ you if you don't add value. So what can you do to reduce the time you give to *Maintenance* and *Crisis Prevention*?

- More scope for delegation of routine matters, perhaps?
- Speedier handling of 'crises'? Fewer and/or shorter meetings? More decisive actions (less procrastination)?
- More ruthless and disciplined strategies/tactics for handling interruptions and limiting access to you?
- Refusal to accept other people's monkeys in future?
- A conscious decision to climb out of your 'comfort zone'?

Mode 2: The Task-Scale Analysis
According to this approach, you analyse your activities in terms of where the task has come from. If you think about it, the things you do have a very limited number of origins.

(1) **Boss-Imposed Tasks:** actions assigned to you, ad hoc, by your seniors (not just your immediate boss). In most cases such tasks are obligatory, but there may be room for negotiation if you can persuade your senior that the task could be handled more effectively by someone else, or that its priority should be down-graded (so that it doesn't interrupt your other activities, or that part of it should be delegated elsewhere (to one or more of your own staff, or even to other people altogether). Bear in mind, however, that jobs given to you by your seniors (especially by people *very* senior to you) help to increase your visibility in the organization, and

should therefore be accepted with alacrity even when they do cause you some inconvenience.

(2) **System-Imposed Tasks**: activities arising from the regular demands and routines of your role, like the completion of weekly returns, budget forecasts, health and safety statistics, and quarterly progress reports. In general, these processes are also obligatory, but again there is scope for performance improvement. What would happen, for example, if you were to stop producing your monthly fly-paper figures? Maybe these results once served a useful purpose (hidden deep in the mists of antiquity), but now they don't and nobody has bothered to tell you. Why not prepare your figures, as usual, but *don't send them to anybody* and wait until one of the usual recipients asks you for them. If they do, you will know that you must continue with this task, at least for the time being (though it is conceivable that the person demanding the figures from you is equally clueless about their rationale but continues to adopt a 'jobs-worth' mentality).

More seriously, to what extent can System-Imposed Tasks be delegated to others? How far can less time be allocated to them by, for example, simply recording significant changes in the position rather than supplying a comprehensive reworking of data? Can some routine activities be performed less frequently: monthly instead of weekly, quarterly instead of monthly? Think of the time you could save if you just did something 12 times a year instead of 52, or four times a year instead of 12.

(3) **Subordinate-Imposed Tasks**: actions arising from requests (and demands) initiated by subordinates, when they ask for **Advice**, **Information** or **Decisions**. This book's sections on preventing and managing

interruptions, on delegation and on monkey-training, have all proposed several techniques for pushing back this particular tide. Suffice to say, here, that the worst thing you can do (for both your staff and yourself) is freely to hand out *solutions* when your subordinates come to you with *problems*. If they have problems, they must learn to solve these problems themselves, and it is your job to help them learn, not to prevent them from learning.

(4) **Customer-Imposed Tasks:** whoever your 'customers' are, whether they be internal or external, they are bound to make inroads on your time. In a sense, such approaches are welcome, even when your 'customer' has a complaint, because it is well known in customer-service circles that the majority of dissatisfied customers don't complain: they simply take their business elsewhere, if they can, and you may never know what you did wrong. If a customer complains, and you handle the complaint efficiently and effectively, you can tie the customer more closely to you. So feedback from your 'customers' has to be welcome, and if it's favourable feedback then it's doubly welcome. At the same time, it may be that your 'customers' would get even better service if they approached the relevant member of your team directly, instead of you. Delegation of at least some 'customer-care' functions may therefore be advisable from every standpoint: your 'customers' are even happier, your staff have more fulfilling roles and you liberate some time for some value-added priorities.

(5) **Self-Imposed Tasks:** actions which are distinctive because they are undertaken voluntarily and require a high degree of self-motivation. Self-imposed tasks are concerned with adding value or managing change; they include, more specifically, method

166

improvements and reorganization, personal development process (like reading and course/conference
participation), and performance review for your
staff.

Should your analysis reveal that negligible amounts of
time are spent on Self-Imposed Tasks, then a scrutiny of
the other categories of Task is needed because it will be
obvious that you are not adding genuine value to your
organization.

Mode 3: The Time-Scale Analysis
The third system for classifying your activities pre-sup-
poses that time itself can be subdivided into relevant
groups.

(1) **Administration Time** covers time spent on clerical
and routine work, form-filling, data manipulation,
completion of expense returns, counter-signature of
documents, and so forth. Many of these activities
could and should be done by others. The danger is
that we retain some of these processes, on some
semi-rational pretext or other, but in reality because
they make up a 'comfort zone' of familiar tasks
which give us the illusion of progress, dynamism,
and personal involvement through 'keeping on top
of the job'.

(2) **Communications Time** includes, as the category suggests, the receipt of instructions from seniors, attendance at progress meetings, networking and
lobbying, and report-writing. Some activities under
this heading are unavoidable (spending time with
your boss and other seniors is to your advantage),
but a few can be delegated so that, for example, you
send a representative to specific meetings (or your

team stops attending altogether).

(3) **Operations Time** refers to non-managerial activities. A sales manager may spend some time selling; an engineering manager may take out his spanner; a chief accountant may add up columns of figures. For individuals newly embarked on a managerial career, some combination of 'managerial' and 'operational' duties is inevitable, but if further advancement into managerial roles is sought, then it is the managerial dimension which has to grow. Operations Time can be reduced by a more diligent attitude towards delegating responsibility and authority to qualified staff; it may also respond to a refusal to accept monkeys temptingly placed as bait by others who are only too anxious to opt out from their legitimate duties.

(4) **Supervision Time** embraces things like giving orders to staff (even when the orders are disguised as 'requests' or 'suggestions'), inspecting their work, coaching, instructing, listening and motivating. Participation at 'team meetings' or 'team briefing' sessions counts as Supervision Time, as does any activity associated with MBWA.

(5) **Wasted Time** does *not* mean the hours you spend at meetings led by others. [If this is a difficulty for you, read the section in this book on how to participate constructively at meetings.] Wasted Time simply means the accumulation of those moments when you sit at your workstation without doing anything or thinking about anything in particular, but simply gazing blankly into space. If you work at home, Wasted Time will include watching children's television, looking out of the window, or supervising the window-cleaner. We recognize that some Wasted Time is therapeutic – it can be helpful to 'switch off' occasionally – but it can be counter-productive when

it does little more than disguise systematic procrastination.

(6) **Executive Time** is given to planning, exploring, creating, thinking and deciding. The proportion of time spent here will account for the extent to which you add value. If you spend only about five minutes a week on Executive Time, then it follows that you must do little or no thinking about your role and therefore your potential for performance improvement is negligible.

LEARNING FROM THE RESULTS AND YOUR ANALYSIS

Once you've found the mode of analysis which fits your needs and your situation, you will be able to allocate approximate percentages to each of the categories within the mode. This should demonstrate precisely where things are going wrong and what you must do in order to put them right.

Of course, whatever approach you use, it is founded on the presumption that **there are some things you should be doing with your time** and therefore some things which you shouldn't be doing. Indeed, the principles behind time management rely on the need to become *more efficient*, thereby releasing time which will enable you to become *more effective*. You become more effective if you **add value,** and you add value by focusing on:

1. *In the Value-added Analysis* **Performance Improvement** and **Change Management.**
2. *In the Task-Scale Analysis* **Self-Imposed Tasks** (plus a few **Boss-Imposed Tasks** in order to enhance your visibility).

3. *In the Time-Scale Analysis Executive Time* such as planning, exploring, creating, thinking and deciding.

So, what can you do? The answer is to go back and read the book again, concentrating on those pointers which will be of maximum benefit to you in generating opportunities for **Performance Improvement** and **Change Management** through **Self-Imposed Tasks** and **Executive Time**.

And if you're still not sure where to look, complete the Activity Analysis Checklist and the other Checklists on the next few pages.

Good luck.*

*Though it isn't in fact luck you need, but skill, insight, persistence and discipline. Remember Gary Player's dictum: *'The more I practise, the luckier I get.'*

Activity Analysis Sheet

	Time Spent		Action which can be taken to review/ change the situation
	hrs/mins	% of total	
How much time did you spend . . .			
1. Anticipation and Pre-planning? . . . dealing with things that were unexpected? . . . dealing with things that you expected or had anticipated but for which you had made no preparations? . . . dealing with things which you had expected, thought about and for which you made some tangible preparations and plans?			
2. Sources of Demands . . . responding to the demands of your immediate boss or of other senior people? . . . responding to the demands of colleagues on the same level as yourself? . . . responding to the demands of your immediate subordinates and other 'junior' staff? . . . responding to the demands of the 'system'?			
3. Contacts . . . on your own? . . . with your immediate subordinates? . . . with your immediate boss? . . . with other people?			

171

Activity Analysis Sheet

How much time did you spend . . .	Time Spent		Action which can be taken to review/ change the situation
	hrs/mins	% of total	
4. Location . . . in your own 'office'? . . . in other people's 'offices'? . . . on sites and plants? . . . travelling? . . . other?			
5. Paperwork . . . handling paperwork? . . . writing/reading letters and memos? . . . dealing with other paperwork?			
6. Urgency and Crises . . . dealing with issues that were urgent? . . . dealing with things that were urgent but not important?			

Activity Analysis Sheet

How much time did you spend . . .	Time Spent		Action which can be taken to review/change the situation
	hrs/mins	% of total	
7. Specialist & Managerial Activities . . . dealing with specialist matters for which you were trained? . . . dealing with managerial issues not immediately connected with people? . . . dealing with people management issues (i.e., recruiting, disciplining, training, counselling, supporting, directing, leading, etc.)? . . . dealing with organizational and procedural administration?			
8. Personal Areas . . . on things of largely personal interest (incl. meetings which, whether you went or not, depended solely on you)? . . . on coffee and meal breaks and other breaks for personal needs? . . . training, educating or developing yourself? . . . on social activities made necessary by the job?			
9. Other Aspects of Importance to you			

ACTIVITY ANALYSIS

GUIDE QUESTIONS

1. What proportion of the activities could have been avoided (or modified) by improved anticipation on my part or on someone else's part?

2. What proportion of my time was spent on 'minor episodes' (less than 5 minutes)?

3. What proportion of my time was logged as 'interruptions'? Which of these should be reclassified (e.g., training subordinate; where an interruption began another 'activity')?

4. What proportion of/how many activities lasted longer than was useful?

5. What proportion of the duration of each activity or incident was I able to influence (e.g., stop when *I* wanted to)?

6. What proportion of the activities could have been carried out without my direct participation – without loss of overall effectiveness?

7. What greater proportion of my work activity could and *should* I have delegated to a subordinate?

8. What proportion of my time was spent on activities which didn't seem to make a significant contribution to getting the job done (e.g., travel)?

9. What proportion of my time was spent in 'thinking'
   – creatively?
   – planning the future?

10. What proportion of my time was spent in administrative tasks that I feel should be done by someone else/different grade?

THE MANAGEMENT – CHECKLISTS

MANAGING YOUR OWN WORKSTATION

1. Do you have an adequate filing system?
2. How much time do you lose looking for lost files or incorrectly filed material?
3. If you do your own filing, do you allocate a regular time (e.g. 4.00 p.m. Friday) to keep it up to date?
4. Are you in the habit of filing paper 'in case you need it'?
5. Do you regularly review files, say every year, discarding old material?
6. Do you use your desk as a filing cabinet?
7. If you receive all incoming mail for your unit, do you pass on delegated material immediately? Do you dispose of anything you do not need?
8. Do you allow mail to pile up in your in-tray?
9. Do you have a system for sorting your mail in terms of priority or action?
10. Do you allocate a regular time for activities like dictation?
11. Do your staff gain access to you by coming in at any time or through a booking system?
12. Do you use your desk diary as a planning aid?
13. Is your desk cluttered because you like to keep all papers on current projects on it?
14. Do you constantly waste time looking for pencils, rubbers, rulers, etc.?
15. By adopting a systematic approach to your self-management, are you aware of the positive effect it will have on your staff?

THE MANAGEMENT – CHECKLISTS

COMMUNICATIONS

1. Do you know how many communications you send and receive in a day?
2. Have you considered grouping, delegating or handling them in a different way, making less demand on your time?
3. Are you satisfied with your way of expressing yourself, both in speech and writing, to both staff and your 'customers'?
4. When personally communicating, do you *listen* enough to gain complete understanding? Do you encourage staff to improve their skills of listening?
5. Do you have a polite bur firm way of persuading a visitor to leave?
6. Do you find real communication does not take place, even at meetings? Have you tried to identify barriers to communications and ways of breaking them down?
7. Is communication between sections and individuals poor because they do not meet often enough to understand each other's point of view? How can this be resolved?
8. Have you thought of communicating with people at *their* place of work rather than your own?
9. When using the telephone, do you try to group outgoing calls together, and have another task ready to carry out if kept waiting?
10. Are you clear what each telephone call should achieve and do you have all relevant information ready?
11. When unable to make contact, do you agree a time to phone again, or encourage an interruption by

asking the person to phone back?

12. When communicating by telephone on a complex matter, do you consider writing first with some background information?

13. If you have to make frequent phone contact with someone who is often absent from his desk, can you agree on a time when both of you can clear outstanding issues?

14. Do you indulge in too much social chat on the telephone? Do you have a polite but firm way of ending an excessively long call?

15. Do you consider using telex or fax as part alternative to the telephone?

16. Is your telephone system the most suitable for your needs?

17. By adopting a systematic approach to your self-management are you aware of the positive effect it will have on your staff?

THE MANAGEMENT – CHECKLISTS

PAPERWORK

1. How much time do you spend on various types of paperwork, e.g., letters, memos, forms, returns, agendas, minutes, internal reports, circulars, instructions, trade/technical journals?

2. What benefits do you gain from the above? Should you reduce the amount you read?

3. Do you *scan* written material to decide whether or not to read it?

4. Have you tried to increase your reading speed?

5. Can you share the reading of journals, etc., concentrating yourself on the more relevant ones/articles?

6. Do you carry reading material with you which can be read in unexpected waiting periods or during travelling time?
7. Do you highlight important points to save time when rereading?
8. Do you allow time for self-improvement reading?
9. Do you make the maximum use of standard forms (e.g. incidents/complaints etc.) to avoid repetitive composition?
10. Do you regularly evaluate forms, making improvements where necessary, or scrapping them if they are not serving a purpose?
11. Are you spending too much time on internal memos? Have you considered alternative ways of dealing with internal communication?
12. Are you being as concise as possible in your writing?
13. Do you encourage staff to produce a one page summary of all reports?
14. Are you making full use of word processors, particularly in drafting reports and minutes?

THE MANAGEMENT – CHECKLISTS

INTERRUPTIONS

1. How many interruptions do you receive each day?
2. Are you interrupted because you are too visible?
3. Do you invite interruptions by telling staff that your door is always open?
4. Are you afraid of missing something by not dealing with interruptions as they occur?
5. Do some people regularly interrupt several times a day? Can you arrange to meet when several matters can be dealt with together?

6. What do you do when interrupted in the middle of a task?
7. Do people come to you because they know you like to be helpful?
8. If you are asked for advice, help or information, are you the right person to give it?
9. When asked for information because you are head of the unit/section, can you give them the choice of supplying the information yourself in, say, 2 hours, or transferring them to a colleague who can deal with them immediately?
10. If there are people who want to tell you or sell you something (which perhaps you should know about), can you make a rule about when you are available?
11. How many interruptions are by people who should not come to you at all? Can you brief them to see the right person?
12. Can someone screen your callers?
13. Should unexpected telephone callers take priority over visitors with an appointment?
14. Has your organization got the most effective telephone system? Has advice been sought from external bodies?
15. Can you arrange for your telephone calls to be interrupted?
16. By adopting a systematic approach to your self-management, are you aware of the positive effect it will have on your staff?

THE MANAGEMENT – CHECKLISTS

INFORMATION

1. Is your regular incoming information in a standard

form (print-outs, weekly/monthly summaries)? Can its presentation be improved in any way?

2. Do you receive more information than you need, and can you take steps to reduce it or be removed from the circulation list?

3. Do you feel that you are not getting enough information, due to inadequate/poor communication? Is there anything you can do to help?

4. Are you subject to delay in receiving information? If so, can the information be on a more selective basis, but delivered to agreed timetables?

5. Have you developed an effective procedure for follow-up queries on information? Do you have the right contacts to achieve this?

6. Do you automatically file all copies of incoming information? Are there other copies filed elsewhere?

7. If you need to refer frequently to information from a central computerized file, can you use a terminal?

8. Do you and others share information enough, or is there a tendency to hold on to it for various reasons?

9. By adopting a systematic approach to your self-management are you aware of the positive effect it will have on your staff?

THE MANAGEMENT – CHECKLISTS

MEETINGS

1. Is it always clear to you and other staff why a meeting has been called and what it has to accomplish?

2. Do you always ensure that the meeting has been properly convened, agendas produced and sent out, venue checked for availability/suitability, meeting time chosen to suit estimated duration and the

convenience of members?

3. Do you always make sure that the *right number* of people and the *right* people attend, bearing in mind the purpose of meeting?

4. As a participant in the meeting, do you always attend knowing the purpose of the meeting and prepared for the discussion?

5. Do you try to ensure that you come to the meeting with an open mind?

6. When chairing the meeting, do you try to achieve a good balance between your own input and participation from members? Do you try to ensure that the processes within the meeting are effective?

7. Do you sometimes come with a 'hidden agenda' which might conflict with the spirit of the meeting?

8. Do you acknowledge the authority of the chair, speak too much (or too little)?

9. Do you sometimes let personal rivalries affect the conduct and effectiveness of meetings?

10. Do you ever consider cancelling a regular meeting if there is very little to discuss?

11. Do you ensure that all your meetings end with everyone agreed on the decisions reached and committed to implement them?

12. Have you considered the most effective ways of taking and producing minutes/records of meetings and Action Notes?

13. Do you discuss with staff, perhaps for a few minutes at the end of meetings, ideas on saving time at future meetings?

14. By adopting a systematic approach to your self-management are you aware of the positive effect it will have on your staff?

TIME MANAGEMENT – CHECKLISTS

PLANNING

1. When planning which jobs to do first in the day, do you choose:
   - the routine tasks?
   - the difficult jobs?
   - the unpleasant jobs?
   - the creative jobs?
   - the multi-stage jobs?
2. Do you make sure that some of the jobs on your list are connected with your key priorities?
3. Do you use a 'things-to-do' list for each day? If so, what kind of jobs are left unfinished at the end of the day?
4. When using a 'things-to-do' list, have you thought of writing down how long you think each job will take, thus producing a time budget?
5. Are you making use of desk diaries, personal time planners and wall charts to aid your planning?
6. How do you cope with deadlines?
7. How do you cope with complex jobs? Do you try to produce a series of action plans, each covering one aspect of the job, and each containing a list of manageable activities?
8. Do you try to anticipate busy periods by working at pressure to remove any backlog of work so as to 'clear the decks'?
9. Do you frequently complete fewer jobs than you plan to do each day? If so, do you know why?
10. Do you believe that most of your job is responding to other people and events, and that planning your time is impossible?
11. If most of your job is reacting to people and events,

what do you do whilst waiting for each event to occur?

12. Do you make use of the time you are kept waiting for an appointment or if a meeting is cancelled by carrying a small task or having a journal to read?

13. Do you sometimes suffer from procrastination? If so, have you thought of setting yourself some realistic targets in your diary, and making sure you meet them?

14. Are you aware of Parkinson's Law – 'Work expands to fill the time available'?

15. Do you know when your mind is at its most active, and can you plan to do the most exacting jobs in these periods?

16. At the end of the day/week do you review your plan and consider where the time went? Do you keep a work diary from time to time to update yourself on where the problems lie?

17. By adopting a systematic approach to your self-management are you aware of the positive effect it will have on your staff?

Management of time – Action Plan

Taking into consideration:
- the context of my job
- my personality type
- my time problems

I have the energy and am committed to tackling the following time management problems:

Problem	How I will overcome this	By (Date)	Result

MANAGERIAL TIME EFFECTIVENESS: ACTIVITY RECORD

Date:_____	Day of Week:_____
Before 9 a.m.	1 p.m.
9 a.m.	2 p.m.
10 a.m.	3 p.m.
11 a.m.	4 p.m.
12 noon	5 p.m. and after

References and Further Reading

Bittel, L. R. *Right on Time: The Complete Guide for Time-Pressured Managers*, Maidenhead: McGraw-Hill, 1991.

Margol, J. and Kleiner, B. H. 'New developments in effective time management.' *Mangement Decision*, Vol. 27, No. 5, 1989, pp. 28–34.

Pedler, M. and Boydell, T. *Managing Yourself*, Aldershot: Gower Publishing, 1990.

Taylor, H. and Cooper, C. L. 'Organizational change: threat or challenge?' *Journal of Organizational Change Management*, Vol. 1, No. 1, 1988, pp. 68–80.

Thomas, P. R. *Time Warrior: Using the Total Cycle Time System to Boost Personal Competitiveness.* New York: McGraw-Hill, 1992.

Read on for details of new editions of the bestselling *Perfect* series now available from Random House Business Books

PERFECT CAREER

Max Eggert

In a world where job opportunities are continually shrinking it is more important than ever before to actively manage your career. More time is spent at work than in any other activity, so it is vital to make sure that you are following the correct path.

Perfect Career adjusts the balance in your favour, first by helping you to make a thorough analysis of your skills, experiences and values, and then providing practical strategies to enable you to achieve your career ambitions.

£6.99   1844131459

PERFECT CV

Max Eggert

Whether you're applying for your first job or planning an all-important career move, your CV is the most potent strike weapon in your armoury. This classic, bestselling book is a concise and invaluable guide that gives you the blueprint for the perfect CV. It shows you clearly and quickly how to present you and your skills and experience in the best possible way – and how to avoid the many easily-made mistakes which swiftly antagonize potential employers.

£6.99   1 8441 3144 0

PERFECT INTERVIEW

Max Eggert

Perfect Interview is comprehensive, but concise and to-the-point. It shows you quickly and clearly how to present yourself and your skills in the best possible way at an interview. Packed with success, tips and checklists, it will enable you to make sure the interview goes the way *you* want it to – and that the result is a job offer that's satisfactory to both you and your new employer.

£6.99   1 8441 3143 2